Shiny New Science Vagina

How I Got My Vagina 33 Years Late

By Marissa Alexa McCool

With

Bethany Turner

Hontas Farmer

Melina Rayna Barratt

Also By Marissa Alexa McCool

The PC Lie: How American Voters Decided I Don't Matter

False Start

Silent Dreams

Voice in the Dark

Passing Cars: The Internal Monologue of a Neurodivergent Trans

Girl

Once Unspoken: A Series of Monologues From the Previously

Unheard

Copyright © 2018, It's a Shameful Thing, Lobsterhead! LLC All Rights Reserved

ISBN-13: 9781791730048

To Aiden, Devyn, Isaac

Michael, Kieran, Kaitlin

Donna, Kenny, Pru, Zizi

LaLa, Callie, Ari, Bethany

And a special thank you to

Marya Hornbacher and Dr. Martinez

How Did I Get *Here?*

I grabbed the metal bar above the bed like I was doing a pull-up as they gently snipped the stitches sewing the bolster into my five-day-old vagina.

Five days earlier, the day after my 33rd birthday, I was admitted to the Mayo Clinic at six in the morning for gender confirmation surgery. A week before that, I'd had my pre-op consultation, which consisted of seven appointments between the hours of 7:45am and 3:15pm. It was quite similar to the four appointments back in January when I had my initial consultation, which had a five hour break between the third and fourth appointments and saw me come down with the flu before the end of the day.

June, 2017 was when I moved to Minnesota, immediately after graduating from the University of Pennsylvania in May; partially because of the legal protections on a local and state level provided for trans people in the state; unique to most areas in the country. Three months before that, I'd survived being stuck in a snowstorm to eventually make my court date to legally change my name Once I'd paid the $115 to file, gotten fingerprinted, published the change in two newspapers, and acquired the resources for both the name and gender marker change on my driver's license. I was able to alter, one-by-one, my social security card, birth certificate, bank account, credit cards, voter registration, third cousin's email forwarding address, and spam text messages from dating sites.

November, 2016, around the time I published my first book/rant under my real name, my university changed my name on all documents and web connections with only one question asked: "Are you transgender?" One month prior, October 3rd, 2016, I'd screamed "I'm transgender, fuck you!" in the face of a hate preacher on campus while skipping the first class I'd later come out in to counterprotest. Two months before that date, on August 21st, 2016, I'd married my trans husband under our dead identities for the sake of the 10 percent of the attendees, i.e. our family members, who weren't yet aware that we were both trans and I'd already been on hormones for two months. Those were acquired when I met with the only doctor at student health who was knowledgeable about transgender people at a university with trans-inclusive student health insurance and a population of 42,000 students on July 13th, 2016. When I'd learned about the trans-inclusive healthcare at Penn, that was just over a year after I was sexually assaulted twice in one week after spending several months slowly coming to terms with my gender identity and expressing it in specifically safe places.

It had taken me seven months to work up the courage to go to the doctor. When the Pulse Massacre in Orlando took place in June of 2016, that pushed me over the edge. The list of victims was published, and the second name on the list had the name McCool. I realized that if I'd been there at the bar that night, amongst my community but living in secret, and I'd passed away, 99 percent of the people in my life would've remembered the wrong person, the wrong name, the wrong gender. They would've remembered the shell I was in while not revealing that I was dead inside. They would've remembered an actor, because Marissa was who I'd been since I got the name.

And that, of course, was eleven years after I first got the name Marissa after participating in a ploy to ward off a jealous boyfriend by pretending to be a girlfriend of the bothered ex. I was eighteen, raised in a conservative, elitist school district, and the only term I had for myself after realizing I liked dressing up and being called Marissa was "drag queen." I wouldn't learn what transgender was until eleven years later, when someone corrected me on that term in a Facebook community, and this journey truly began.

What An Objectively Shitty Choice This Would Be (If It Was One)

There's a joke in the trans community that revolves around the stages of admitting being trans to yourself. It goes, more or less, like this:

-I like wearing these clothes and expressing myself differently, but I don't think I'm transgender.

-Okay, so I might be transgender, but I don't think I'll ever go on hormones.

-Okay, so I'll go on hormones, but I don't think I'll ever publicly transition.

-Okay, so I'll publicly transition, but I don't think I'll ever get the surgery.

-Okay, I really want the surgery.

(Note: There isn't one specific "trans surgery" though that's what most people tend to ask within a minute of meeting you.)

The extreme caution in taking the steps to transition arises from fear; not just fear of society at large, but of the legalized discrimination in America that affects everything in our lives, from housing to medical care. Being transgender in this country involves a lot of gaslighting, including from the internalized transmisogyny you've acquired over the course of your life living in a culture that only represents trans identity as a punchline or a plot twist for a serial killer. When a majority of the population will respond aggressively to your existence, refuse to let you use the bathroom, sexually assault or murder you and then use Trans Panic (otherwise known as freaking out from learning a person is trans or realizing you slept with a trans person and being overwhelmed with fear about anyone else finding out) as a defense, and let you die after refusing to treat you in an emergency, living your life as a fully out transgender person is a terrifying proposition, even in the "friendlier" areas. You never know where the next person who listens to anti-trans propaganda and takes it literally will be.

Every year in November, we read off hundreds of names during the Trans Day of Remembrance, a litany of trans people who were murdered for being trans. It's particularly bad in Brazil, but enough American names pop up every year that remind us that if anyone harms us, most of the time there won't even be an investigation, let alone justice. Even as I write this, there's the possibility of there being a serial killer in Florida, mostly Jacksonville, targeting trans women of color, and despite five deaths this year, not much has been done about it. While our experience of distrusting law enforcement isn't equivalent to that of people of color, it does have parallels that make us do anything possible to avoid contact with the police.

That, of course, is also only one of the public dangers of existing while trans. Coming home or going to school doesn't make anything easier, most of the time. The streets are filled with LGBTQ homeless youth kicked out by religious or otherwise-intolerant parents, while many more live in the closet for fear of violence, losing their home, or having their college funding removed. For older trans people, fear of your partner or spouse leaving you is a heavy cloud over deciding to come out to the person who is supposed to love you through better or worse. I know one trans person specifically whose ex-wife had it written into her new husband's wedding vows that he will not turn into a woman.

Losing your children if you're already a parent, especially if you split custody, is a huge risk as well. Recently, a court ruled that another trans person I know would only be allowed to see her children if she presented as her deadname and identity. Essentially, trans people who make the decision to live openly have to assume every person and place is hostile toward us, until explicitly proven otherwise. Even some LGBTQ+ support groups aren't at all welcoming to the T in the acronym; most notoriously, this includes cisgender female lesbians who systematically engage in bullying, doxxing, and encouraging trans people to commit suicide, also known as Trans-Exclusionary Radical Feminists, or TERFs. It's hard to know if any place outside of your own home is safe, and, as I've said, even home isn't universal for a terrifying percentage of the trans population.

Despite all of that, I made the decision that I would rather live authentically in a dangerous climate than pretend to be someone I wasn't for any longer than I already had. I am Marissa. I'm a queer, polyamorous, transgender woman, and I just had bottom surgery. Two years and two months after going on hormones, and 15 years after first getting my name.

Race to the Vagina

I never explicitly hated my penis.

This is one of a number of myths that surround the trans community, and it isn't helped by "clever" comedians who make jokes about us "cutting it off." Even when I was finally coming to terms with who I am, it wasn't about me having a penis. That did change the longer into transition I was, but we often spend a great deal of time clearing up myths about trans people. That, and answering questions about our genitals upon meeting someone for the first time. Even now that I've had surgery, it never ends.

Going through with the surgery had very little to do with sex. Sex was one of the aspects of having a penis I didn't mind too terribly much, but every time I'd meet a new person who didn't know me pre-transition and saw me entirely as a woman, that first moment of intimacy was always anxiety-inducing. My internal monologue was always bound up in hoping that she/they didn't think of me differently once they'd confirmed me being trans, even though they already knew, and wondering if seeing this part of me made them think of me as less of a real woman when everything else matched up. Society has a way of ruining even the most positive moments we experience as trans people.

Having sex in the "traditional" manner because more and more difficult the longer I was on hormones. By about the 18-month mark, there was only one area that felt even remotely sensitive anymore. Fortunately, that's the area doctors make the clitoris out of, so there are some silver linings to the process for most people who go through the procedure.

Having an orgasm in the "old" way became excruciatingly difficult after a year or so, and didn't produce anything in the process, so at least cleanup wasn't an issue. My husband is a trans man and has a vagina, so we still engaged in PIV intercourse as we both transitioned. However, erections were more troublesome to attain. Maintaining one for more than a few minutes was a factor, and I would often lose energy quickly as well.

As my clothing style began to take on its own identity, some of the clothes I really liked also were tight around the waist area. Some trans women take part in what's called tucking, or essentially pushing their penis back between their legs to remove any bulging. This method was never comfortable for me, so I was left with the decision of wearing something I really liked and risking the bulge being noticeable, or finding a way to cover it up for the sake of my comfort and safety. I was never confronted about it; it was almost entirely self-induced, but that bulge's presence always had the potential to ruin a day.

Going to the bathroom posed challenges as well. By the time I was exclusively using the women's room, I also was sitting down to pee regardless of being at home or in public (I'd never dream of standing to pee in public in a women's bathroom, even if I ever wanted to). There was still that moment of sitting down, and then adjusting in order to achieve the necessary result, and that alone made me uncomfortable. That was one of the few times I'd engage in any method of tucking, but that was mostly hiding it under my closed legs so I didn't have to see it, as well as trying to make the sounds coming from my stall as similar to the others as possible. Yes, anxiety and social fear do bring those thoughts to your mind.

I was taking the steps to undergo GCS even as I was unsure about wanting or needing it. The fear was as much about going through the physical process as it was about the circumstances. The pain, something that I'd lost the ability to tolerate since starting to transition, was a factor. The time off I'd have to take from work also needed to be considered. The debts that would accumulate from one less income for a significant amount of time came into play. As well as the fact that I'd never had surgery, or even been in the hospital for that matter. Never broke a bone, never had stitches, so my medical experience was extremely limited. Having no health insurance for most of my twenties didn't help either.

I also wondered if my husband would lose interest in me. He generally only dates cis men, and he doesn't appear to be interested in expanding that horizon. His preference for cis men and trans women made me fear that if I lost the appendage that kept me in the genital preference category of his choice, would he stop being attracted to me?

Also, as a trans person, if you don't have to want surgery, you're no less valid for not having had it yet or wanting it at all. I didn't want to be accused of perpetuating that stereotype that all trans women wanted GCS and that was the required step of "becoming" a woman. I certainly don't believe it's a step that all trans women should have to or want to take. It's expensive, difficult to get approved for, invasive, dangerous, and the waiting lists are normally years long.

What it came down to in my case was that I wanted a vagina. Internally, even as I had sex with a penis, in my mind I was envisioning myself being penetrated by the other person with my eyes closed. I stopped using words associated with genitalia of the penile persuasion to describe myself in any way, as it made me increasingly uncomfortable. It had to go, even if my attitude toward it wasn't entirely negative.

And, on top of everything else, I had the opportunity.

Many trans women don't get the chance at all. When I was at university in Philadelphia, every hospital in the area that performed the surgery had a three-to-five year waiting period. But my public activism put me in touch with a number of trans people on a regular basis, and one of them told me about the newly-opened gender clinic at the Mayo Clinic in Rochester, Minnesota. As it happened, I was already planning on moving to Minnesota upon graduation; and with the program being so new, the wait lists would not yet be years long. I had my first appointment to discuss the surgery with a social worker at Mayo in June of 2017, and had the surgery in September of 2018. That included the necessary waiting period of having publicly and socially transitioned for at least a year. I acquired the necessary recommendation letter from a psychiatrist, and it took two months for the Mayo Clinic to receive it in order to continue. All told, it took about 15 months from the start of the process to the surgery itself.

I felt an obligation to get the surgery because so many others either didn't have the opportunity or couldn't afford to take it. I felt an obligation to those who went through it in the 90s and before when most people didn't know what a trans person was, and you had to live as your gender for two years socially before they'd even let you have hormones. For those I knew who went through it at a more socially difficult time without any help, any assistance, any support, there was an element of guilt weighing on me for being so scared when my obstacles couldn't compare to theirs.

Finally, with the U.S. president systematically removing as many of our community's rights as he possibly could while also making it ever easier to "legally" discriminate against us, I feared that soon, he'd make it illegal for insurance companies to cover our HRT or surgeries, or ban the procedure from being done in hospitals, or any of the other evangelical baseless asskissing he's done.

It was a race to the vagina against Trump. And I won.

Ask "When's Your Birthday" One More Time!

Sarah had broken up with me only a few days beforehand, so my emotional tenderness was even higher than usual.

Figuring out that Devyn, my long-term partner, and I needed to get a ride down was a huge ask, seeing as Rochester is about 75 minutes away from where we live with my husband Aiden and my two children, Michael and Kieran. I'm really glad we decided to go down the night before. At the Mayo Clinic, when you're about to get surgery, you don't learn your admission time until you call a number between 8:15 p.m. and midnight the night before, so there's no time to plan. Had we decided to go down the morning of, we would've been leaving around 4:45am at the latest. Granted, I was going to be sleeping most of the day anyway, but getting up that early is no simple task.

The reason we needed a ride though? We'd been counting on my now ex-partner, who had an SUV which required no bending to get into. My husband drives a VW beetle, and I have a VW Jetta with a manual transmission, which nobody else in my house can use. When my partner broke up with me a week before the surgery, it was one more thing for which I had to plan, and on only a week's notice. We'd need to figure out a way home, too.

This was the kind of stress I didn't need going into such an emotionally volatile situation. My body had pretty much been shutting down in preparation for the procedure. My energy was tanked, my libido was dead, and my patience for dealing with people was non-existent. I canceled all my plans in the days leading up to the surgery. The night before, I could barely sleep from the anticipation and anxiety of the procedure looming.

Internally, I was questioning whether or not I should go through with it. The pain, long recovery, and emotional exhaustion were definitely factors, but finances were also an unfortunate reality, even though I had it better than most, as my insurance was covering it.

I'd lost my job about six weeks prior, which ended the short-term disability benefits along with it that I'd be receiving from my employer. I'd been at that job nine months, during which I was subjected to repeated misgendering and mistreatment from supervisors. Finally, I walked out when it became too much. Minnesota initially rejected my unemployment claim, considering my decision to walk out not being due to circumstances that would motivate an average worker to do so. I knew I needed to fight against that, so I appealed their decision.

Appealing the decision was a lengthy and draining process. For two hours, I explained why repeated and intentional misgendering created a hostile work environment, especially given that these supervisors didn't know me pre-transition. A decision would be made after the teleconference, but it had been on August 28th, and no ruling had been made. Because of the circumstances, a few friends of mine had started a GoFundMe in my name.

I felt guilty over asking for financial support, as I knew there were many trans people just trying to survive or eat. And I was aware that having a media platform gave me access to a larger audience than many others have. But it wasn't realistic to think that I could get a job for a month and then take six weeks off. It's hard enough to get hired as a trans person as it is. Therefore, I accepted the fundraiser only under the condition that it was replacing the income I would've been making up until that point and over the duration of the estimated recovery time. I knew I had a responsibility to not take too much from the community. But, at the same time, I live with two partners and two preteen kids, and unemployment was still up in the air. I had to swallow my pride and accept the help.

As I did so, the podcasting community really came out in full force to aid me in the process. Several people got together in secret and recorded an episode specifically for me. It was 49 minutes of people pouring their souls about me. I'm still beyond disbelief that it happened. I went from being invisible to having a decent-sized audience nearly overnight, and I don't think I ever adjusted from feeling like nobody knew or cared who I was. One day, I was a podcaster that a few people knew of, and then, after screaming in a hate pastor's face and writing a book after the election, I had an audience to whom I felt responsible.

Fortunately, once we found out my admission to the hospital would be at 6am, we were already most of the way to Rochester, and the hotel was right across the street. I'd never seen a hotel room so small, but we weren't going to be there for very long anyway. It reminded me of when I lived in an apartment the size of a postage stamp when I made the foolish decision to be on my own at 18.

Admission at the Eisenberg Center felt a little like a TSA screening. Devyn and I both had suitcases, since the hospital stay was going to be a week long, and we were walking along a white marble floor with our luggage rolling behind us. Then we got to stand in an admissions line while people had to give their name and date of birth. When you have appointments at the Mayo Clinic, you're asked to give your birthdate more times than you have birthdays. This was no exception, and every single person I encountered asked what procedure I was having that day.

Once we were finally admitted, we sat down in a waiting room that once again reminded me of an airport. The notification board on the screen with patient numbers and procedure status updates was similar to the arrival/departure boards you see when you finally get through security. Actually, one of the secondary benefits of GCS to which I was looking most forward was not getting the customary trans groin pat down session. I traveled a lot in 2017 for activism, and it got to the point that I'd just put my arms in the air because I knew what was coming. The choices were to go stealth - i.e. - dress down and "pass" as your assigned gender at birth - or present as who you are and inevitably show up on the body scan. Once it got to the point that I could no longer stealth with the size of my chest, the pat-downs were even more regular. If I managed to never have to feel a TSA agent's hands repeatedly swiping across my genitalia ever again, it would be too soon. During the very last one I had, en route to California to give a speech, the agent asked if I'd like to be "rescanned as a man." Ugh. I know the intentions were good, but that's still a dagger to the heart. I opted to just get the pat down and be done with it. Never again. Now nothing will show there that isn't meant to be in the binary cisnormative world of airport security.

My name was called, I repeated my birthday and what procedure I was getting, and we were given some wet wipes and a boxy purple gown to change into. The gown fit like a 1970s NFL player's pads, and I realized what was happening was my first moment involving the phrase "sponge bath." Because of my limited interaction in the medical community and never having been hospitalized, I'd never encountered one of those before, and it was far different than what the wording "sponge bath" suggested. I'd always pictured a giant bathtub and nurses with sponges.

The gown being purple was also a nice touch; due to my purple hair, my nickname is "The Purple Amazon" I worked in a suit store for four years pre-transition, which had the obvious dress code. It wasn't until 15 months later that it occurred to me I no longer had to follow those conservative, outdated expectations. I dyed my hair bright purple, got an immediate nickname for it, and I'd only altered it twice; spending a month with red hair, and another with blue-black. Even once I cut a bunch of my long, thick strands off to go with the trans/lesbian side-shave cliche, I'd kept the non-shaved part purple. I was never able to get away from it for very long.

We were supposed to watch some video about recovering in the hospital, which looked like the equivalent of new employee videos, but we were saved by the nurse calling me back. Devyn took all of my luggage and my clothes, and that was the last I'd see of them for a while. Unfortunately, I had to delay the process for a minute because I had to use the bathroom again. The pre-surgery enemas had been a bit too effective, and I was nervous that I'd end up expelling on the table, seeing as I still was then. I took an Ativan from my personal (prescribed) stash to quell the anxiety a bit, but almost immediately asked for something else. They told me once I had the IV in that they'd include something to calm my nerves, at least after I told them what procedure I was getting again.

Walking into a room that reminded me of an ER, I lay down on a hospital bed and, again, confirmed my birthdate and the procedure I was getting. The nurse closed the curtain and made some small talk, trying to lighten up my visible nervousness, I imagine, and then Dr. Martinez and his team came through to introduce themselves, at least after I told him my birthdate and what procedure I was getting. Furthermore, members of the anesthesia team came in to introduce themselves, and

I gave each one of them my name, and of course my birthdate and what procedure I was getting. One of the anesthesiologists enjoyed my sense of humor while the other put the IV in, the latter quipping that once I stopped grimacing from the IV insertion that the hard part was over. I laughed at that, since I sincerely doubted the IV would be the hardest part of this procedure, which I had to confirm again. Then the first of the anesthesiologist referred to me as "he."

It's not like you get randomly assigned surgeries, right? And even if you did, you were around to hear me confirm the procedure I was having at least 48 times. Plus, my name is freaking Marissa. That has never been challenged as a gender neutral name, as far as I'm aware. I corrected him verbally, "she." I didn't think he heard me, so I got his attention and said, "I'm not a 'he'." He did apologize, but at the best hospital in the country, especially for the procedure I was about to endure, which I had to confirm again, that should be something you don't fuck up.

I wasn't expecting to be conscious long enough to see the operating room. I figured they'd slip me the cocktail before proceeding, but sure enough, there I was, and that was pretty intimidating. I even got to grab onto a bar overhead as they swung me from the gurney to the table and then, asked me to confirm my birthdate and what procedure I was getting. Waiting for the cliche of "count back from 100" from one of the doctors around me, I just tried to not feel so that a physician at the Mayo Clinic had misgendered me two minutes before my vaginoplasty.

The next thing I knew, I was vaguely aware of beeping and different colored numbers on a screen.

That Bolster is Sewn Into Where?!

Today I easily got a good four or five inches on my dilation. Depth had been a concern from someone who had also used this surgeon for her GCS, and while I don't have any AMAB (assigned male at birth) partners, I would be disappointed if I only had an inch to work with for the rest of my life. Especially since my thoughts and desires have been different since the surgery, I'm grateful everything is progressing in a positive manner.

Progress on the first night after surgery, however, was eerily similar to the time I got my wisdom teeth taken out, and that's only because I had no other basis of comparison. I don't remember anything that happened in that dentist's office after the anesthesia, but I was told about sleeping extra in the chair, and then being helped into my dad's maroon Chevy Lumina before I eventually regained consciousness. Lying on the bottom futon of the bunk bed in my room, I was playing with the gauze in my mouth before I had a moment of panic and quickly tried to tongue-rush it back to where it was, just in case that was keeping me from bleeding to death or something.

They let me sleep a little longer in the Mayo recovery room as well. I have no reason to believe this is the case, but I imagine they gave me extra anesthesia to alleviate my fear of waking up during the surgery. Eventually, I figured out that I wasn't on some weird podcaster reality show with colored rankings on a screen, and realized that those were my vitals. The room was dark aside from those blue and orange numbers, and I recall telling a nurse about my hilarious delusion, but what I recollect even more than that was the overwhelming sensation of needing to pee.

Being taken to my room and reunited with my partner Devyn, who had been keeping everyone updated on Facebook and would be eagerly awaiting my move back to our home for the next week-ish, added a sense of relief to the confusion and bladder pain. The packing on the surgery area made it feel like my unfortunate appendage was still there, and I kept remembering the vlog of another trans women who I'd interviewed on the podcast. She mentioned being unable to pee back into the catheter before it was removed without sitting on the toilet first, and I kept begging the nurse to put me on the toilet so I could pee. According to Devyn, I also very weakly attempted to pull my catheter out to do so. I must've still been hopped up on the painkillers and anesthesia, because a few days later I'd pull it by accident and ended up doing my impression of an early-morning alarm clock when you've had little sleep.

Despite the catheter, the need to urinate would not go away, so the nurses added a medication for bladder spasms to the small paper cup concoction I'd be swallowing for the next week. Remaining conscious for very long was not much of a possibility, but I do know that Devyn took a picture once I fell back asleep to let everyone know that I'd made it through and was beginning the recovery process. Devyn would mostly remain in charge of my social media for a good four days. Not only did I not trust myself posting, but in that condition, I didn't want to take any chance of getting upset from the usual cavalcade of bullshit and triggers that are plentiful on a Facebook feed. Kavanaugh's confirmation process alone was bringing up a lot of painful memories from my own past, yet even a few hours after major surgery with a bolster sewn inside my new vagina with the dressings on the incision, I felt a pang of guilt for not being active enough. Impostor Syndrome is a bitch.

I'm somewhat certain that Devyn eventually put on *The Scathing Atheist* and *I Doubt it With Dollemore* podcasts respectively. I say somewhat because I don't know if that happened when it was still Thursday night or if it wasn't until Friday that I vaguely recall familiar voices putting me back to sleep with ease. In this case, I'm only reasonably sure of two things: One, every few hours I'd be telling everyone what my birthdate was when a nurse would come in, and two, for the first time in my life, I could just close my eyes and fall asleep at any time of day with no trouble whatsoever. Finally, the power of napping was accessible to my ADHD/always-on-the-move brain!

Bucking the Gold Star System

"Just treat it like a protruding clitoris," I instructed her, holding back the ball of anxiety that extended far beyond what anyone could imagine. "It works pretty much the same."

She was a cisgender lesbian and had never been with anyone AMAB before. A "gold star lesbian," as some have been known to call it. She was curvy, androgynous, and took control, so I was attracted instantly. Don't judge me; I have a type. A very specific, alluring type.

Things were getting hot and heavy for the second time. On our first date, where they had progressed to a certain point but stopped, my underwear area was all but ignored on my end, and I was perfectly fine with that. Not getting the one part of me involved that didn't match up with everything else was never a bother, and sometimes it was a preference. Now, here we were: a flash-in-the-pan lesbian lust-filled romance that was going "all the way," and even though I'd been open about being trans from the beginning, there's still that devastating internal fear. "What if she stops thinking of me as a woman when she sees it?"

In the short term, it was a relative victory. For someone who had never seen a penis before, she got the idea pretty quickly, and though I couldn't manage to have penetrative sex for very long, I was more than happy to use my tongue for as long as it took to keep her satisfied. However, only a few days later, shortly after I'd left Thanksgiving dinner early to see her, I got the "I think I moved too fast/not ready for a relationship/etc" text, which sucked but is also an unfortunate reality for a lot of trans people. We are often, for lack of a better term, "experiments." She was 23, in college, and had never been with a non-cis lesbian before. She tried it out, and therefore could move on from her curiosity. She was dating someone else within a few weeks according to Instagram, and if that hadn't already happened to me on multiple occasions, it probably would've pissed me off more than it did.

Dating while trans is a double-edged sword. If you're open about being trans right away, you risk being flooded with chasers and inappropriate questions from someone you've just met. Not revealing your trans status right away is downright dangerous, lest you be accused of lying, and at worst you could end up being murdered by someone whose sexuality has been challenged and therefore must kill you in "panic."

I don't think anyone who shares memes that trans people must be upfront about their identity at all times ever takes the dangers we face into consideration. Then again, from the same old responses I see whenever we're pissed that another cis actor is going to get an award for playing a trans role, those who argue these values don't take our perspective into consideration at all whatsoever, so I shouldn't be surprised whenever the same person who posts something like that also makes an Attack Helicopter joke. (By that, I mean someone mocking trans identities by saying "I identify as an attack helicopter." It's been overused to death, but everyone who makes that joke always seem to think they're on the cutting edge of clever social commentary.)

I'm luckier than most. I came out to my then-closeted, then-person I was dating, now-husband in July of 2014 when our game night had a drag theme for the week. He came out around six months later, albeit in his habitual way of dropping information like that on me in a by-the-way fashion (Mentioning it to someone else in a game of Cards Against Humanity while I was present, completely thrown off by the new information). I'd never dated a man in my life, and he'd never dated a woman. I'd be lying if I said that I was instantly comfortable with it, but in truth it didn't take very long. By the time he'd come out to me, I was already in love with him, and my only struggle was lying to myself and pretending I didn't want him to move in with me. I liked breasts, I liked vaginas, and I didn't like facial hair, but those preferences were far less important than the person who loved me, as were my husband's preferences for cisgender men.

My Facebook feed is filled with ex-spouses and partners who weren't so fortunate. I've seen at least three posts whose partners left them after they got GCS, which makes no sense to me. Perhaps it's because my attraction to someone is rarely about what's in their underwear, but how you could suddenly stop loving someone because their genitalia changed is beyond my comprehension. It's unfortunately an all-too-common trope.

My partner Devyn, who did their best to sleep while I slept in that hospital bed through the long first day of recovery, had been following my transition via my podcast, and therefore had a cheat sheet of personal details upon meeting me. There was little to no awkwardness once that chance meeting quickly became romantic and sexual in nature during another trip to Seattle specifically to spend a weekend with them less than a month later. We fell for each other quickly, and a month after my visit, decided that the Minnesota-Seattle distance was going to be too far, and they moved in. This would go down as the only time such a move was successful, as the other two times a partner moved in with me (both times another trans woman), they'd turned out disastrous.

I'm luckier than most. And I never take that for granted.

Can I Pencil You in at 9:18 next May?

My husband and kids (aged 11 and 10) would be arriving sometime Friday evening at the hospital. At this point, Aiden and I had been married for just over two years, together for more than four. Devyn and I had been together for about a year and two months. Whenever I'm on a dating site, it's accurate to say that I'm not "dating" anyone, because both of my relationships in that regard are long past the idea of dating. They're committed, long-term, permanent relationships. Devyn had proposed to me back in June a few months prior to the surgery with the most adorable engagement ring whose emblem was shaped like a bow. Sure, the state only legally recognizes one marriage, but fuck the state anyway. We're essentially three spouses raising two children, except Aiden and Devyn's connection is strictly platonic. They regard each other as spouses regardless, and that's a beautiful thing, not to mention quite fortunate and rare for me, having two emotionally intense relationships that don't clash with each other. It's also a built-in protection system, as anyone I date is aware of there being not one, but two partners who love me watching out. I'd only recently started seeing my long-distance partner Isaac again, and even he knew from experience that communication with the two of them was essential to dating happiness.

My local partner had broken up with me about a week prior to the surgery. It was easily the most amicable breakup I'd ever had, but it had been obvious to me that they were only partially present in the relationship. During the most stressful and terrifying time of my life, I needed someone who was willing to be all there for me as I progressed toward surgery, and they at least admitted they were not able to do that. It hurt, but the breakup was notable only in its lack of notability. I'd had partners who cheated on me the weekend I got home from living somewhere else, left me for a 45-year-old cocaine dealer, moved out behind my back, iced me out to the point of madness while living with them, broken up with me via Facebook after spending the entire relationship afraid that I'd break up with them over Facebook, and various others with extreme and defining endings that left few chances for reconciliation. Amicable was outside the norm for me, as was getting back together with someone after we'd broken up. Isaac and I, however, had a mutual partner who played the both of us against one another and created a fictional account in order to drive the wedge between us. Once we'd figured out what happened, we spent a long time working back to the point of love and trust we'd started with, thus discovering

the X-factor for what went wrong, and I was glad for it.

I'm often asked how ridiculous my Google calendar is.

I wouldn't say I'm codependent on my husband (or Devyn, for that matter), but I've become less willing to do activities that involve me leaving them for longer than an evening. While that isn't exclusively about Carla (I'll explain), that plays a major factor. I also think it's fair to say that I'm extremely affectionate and, though it may be a symptom of autism, my passion doesn't plateau or fade over time. The honeymoon phase never ends for me, and that's likely why a lot of my relationships have faded after the first few months. Their intensity levels off while mine does not. Even while asleep, I cling to Aiden like I'm afraid he's going to leave for good, and every time

Devyn comes home from work in the morning, I insist on hugs and kisses. The same is true for when they leave in the evening. Missing any of those is a cause of stress for me. But one of the concerns of all my partners, as well as my own, was for and about Carla.

To put it simply, every night I dissociate into a six-year-old girl named Carla. It used to be that this personality and conversation would only come out when I was already long asleep and dead to the world, but thanks to the sleep medication I'd started once moving to Minnesota, she was starting to come out as the medicine would kick in, and every single night, her personality developed. I'd named her Sleepy Carla as an homage to standup comedian Mike Birbiglia's routine about the guy who takes over his brain for the night shift, whom he named Sleepy Carl. As more evenings passed where Carla would ask questions or make silly statements or say ridiculously sweet nothings, I dropped the Sleepy from the name. Carla was also a place I could go when my emotional battery was completely drained, and I couldn't handle any more intake of the sensory nature. She's a product of a lot of my sexual trauma, as well as being drugged and molested while I slept on a futon for six weeks after I'd left my marital home when I was 23, but she's a valid part of who I am. Whenever Carla comes out, the attitude of the entire house changes and becomes extremely protective of her. As I have trouble walking or pronouncing words, as well as being overly sensitive and emotional, keeping Carla safe is a priority for my partners. She once tried to chase a bunny in the backyard in the middle of the night while there was snow on the ground. She requires some supervision. She calls Aiden "Daddy," albeit not in the traditional BDSM sense, she calls Devyn "Sai" (gender neutral term for "Sir"), and the kids she calls "Little Girl" and "Little Boy" because, as she once put it, "they're short." And Carla, to say it mildly, LOVES Daddy. She tends to cry whenever he gets up at five in the morning to leave, so being without him at all was hard on all of us. Aiden especially takes watching out for Carla seriously, but the whole house is used to it by now.

A lot of my fear over the impending surgery had come out with Carla, who didn't want to go to the "hostible." The three of us worried what would happen with Carla when she woke up in a strange place while attached to an IV and in considerable pain. Part of the reason Devyn took the entire week off that I'd be in the hospital was to make sure I had a familiar person there at all times, but especially when Carla would arrive. The nature of the painkillers and my sleep schedule, however, had negated a Carla appearance thus far. I'd often wake up enough to give my birthdate, take my medication, listen to Devyn read a chapter from *Where She Went* by Gayle Forman or listen to part of a podcast, and I'd be asleep again.

Aiden arrived with the kids, who immediately attached themselves to whichever piece of technology was the most charged. I wasn't expecting any different, as this is what happened anytime they were at home or around me. I grabbed Aiden by the hand and didn't let him go for a good hour once he'd gotten there. Being away from him was one of the more difficult aspects of recovering in the hospital. Berry Bear, my and Carla's favorite stuffed animal, had kept us cuddle company that we couldn't otherwise get because of the hospital bed, but it wasn't a replacement. I was also getting headaches from having to exclusively sleep on my back. I could manage to turn on my side for a few minutes with the assistance of several pillows between my knees, but it was only long enough to get some blood flowing into my back. The gentle massaging Devyn would do at those points was the closest to heaven this atheist has ever felt.

Earlier on Friday as well, I'd done my first walking session. Yes, getting up to walk is done that quickly. With the use of a podium on which to lean that had wheels, my goal was to make it one lap around the nurse's station, or about 100 feet according to the sign nearby. In my usual overachiever fashion, I'd done two laps. I couldn't tell if the numbness in my back was from the lack of movement, or if they'd given me an epidural to help with the pain like they do with pregnancies. I was certainly fine with the latter if that was the case. Walking at this point was like leaning on the bar when you're really drunk and have spilled a drink on your lap, so your legs are spread to avoid the cold wetness. The walks were slow, with keeping my catheter hung on the podium underdeck. The nurse and Devyn followed me with my IV, making sure I didn't slip and fall in my hospital socks.

That was all the time the hospital gown lasted though, as I quickly exchanged it for the t-shirt dresses and silk nightgown I'd received as gifts to get me through recovery. Consideration for the catheter tube was essential, so long t-shirts that were open on the bottom was a comfortable option and required no tying like a hospital gown. All things considered, it wasn't a bad deal.

Devyn took the kids to the hotel they'd gotten for Aiden to give the two of us some time alone while I recovered. The week off was certainly a blessing for me and Devyn, as our opposite schedules at home rarely allowed us to spend extended periods of time together, but having Aiden in the chair next to me for a night was also something for which I was extremely grateful.

Aiden is a trans man, but he's also on the feminine side of the spectrum, and hides his emotions about as well as bright orange blends into the woods. His look of sheer concern and fear let me know how worried he'd been about me. But while he was scrolling through my phone so I could see the updates Devyn had made on my various social platforms, which were receiving numbers of likes in the 3-400 range. Unlike friends of mine, including author Dharma Kelleher, who had the surgery in 1992, I was fortunate that I didn't have to go through this process alone. My friend Melina, who had the same surgery in the same hospital a year prior, flew up from Florida for the procedure, and was therefore geographically distant from her family during the recovery. People like Dharma who came out in a different era when trans visibility was limited to *The Rocky Horror Picture Show* and sitcom plot twists, I can't even imagine what it must've been like to transition in that atmosphere. The world is hostile enough toward us as it is, and though I'd always been frighteningly naive about living openly when I was younger, I never forgot the bullying for being feminine that dated back to when I was seven-years-old and first called a faggot. Central Pennsylvania, everyone.

My emotional sensitivity was at an all-time high, I was falling asleep nearly every two hours, and the distraction of listening to a sports podcast while my husband held my hand tightly was just what I needed.

Having my laptop with me so I could watch my alma mater's opening game was also a pleasant diversion from the bladder pain, the discomfort of being penetrated 100 percent of the time, and never being sure if the blood and other fluid leaking down my backside was instead a wet bowel movement.

I was desperate to not be a pain in the ass to the nurses. I had to be talked into using the call button to ask for pain medication when I needed it. I'd thought the male overnight nurse was annoyed with me, but it would later turn out that he had my back as much as any of them. Most of the nurses I saw would be consistent cast members throughout my stay at Mayo. I'd also been regaled with the story of how all the rooms had framed pictures of Jesus in them, and Devyn had politely handed it to one of the nurses and asked them to keep it there until I left. I approved of this message.

The nurses were kind enough to provide Devyn with a cot next to the bed so they could sleep beside me instead of across the room. For one night, Aiden also got to enjoy that benefit while holding my hand through most of my unconsciousness. A nurse would come in for meds and to check my blood pressure, after I verified my birthdate, between every 2-4 hours, so I can't say I ever got a full night's sleep. But as much as I do, produce, participate in, travel, and intellectually engage with, the conscious decision to abstain from all of it for an extended period of time was as necessary as it was difficult. The world's issues and online activism were going to have to wait a while for me to be involved again. For that night, it was just me and my husband in our own private room kept dark at the Mayo Clinic while he fell asleep holding my hand as I drifted in and out of consciousness.

You Probably Say "Dilly Dilly" With That Shitty Beer You Like, Bart-O

I mentioned before that I've had difficulties sleeping. Napping has been a near impossibility throughout my life, except maybe when I had the flu for the first time. However, to be able to fold my hands and pass out on the spot? That was so foreign to me that sometimes I fell asleep at the hospital intentionally just because I knew I'd never be in a situation where I could do that again.

Our house has five people, and our bedroom is very bright most of the time. Our next door neighbors are constantly either rebuilding a motorboat, or having 48 kids play soccer at top volume. At the Mayo Clinic, the room was kept mostly dark, everything was quiet when I wasn't giving my birthdate, and the medicine definitely had some drowsy effects. Even after major surgery though, I couldn't get over the guilt of feeling like I was supposed to be doing something. Impostor Syndrome, again.

My competitive nature and strong desire to overachieve at something found its outlet in making sure that I walked more than recommended. An elevator down the hall took us down to the third floor where there was a mini-courtyard. It was still difficult for me to be out there long when others were there. Hypervigilance as a trans person never goes away, even in places like hospitals where doctors who are about to perform your vaginoplasty still misgender you. Old white people terrify me. They may not speak loudly as often, but I know what goes on beneath those ugly grimaces and eye rolls they think are so subtle. They're the same kind that pretend they don't believe a drunken frat boy would try to rape a girl at a party before putting him on the highest court in the land. I'm not interested in soliciting their opinions, even by proxy of quiet appearance.

Feeling like I had to pee constantly, I'd sometimes still go sit on the toilet in case I was going to have a bowel movement. Having never been in that situation before, it was impossible to tell the difference between gas, cramps, and anything moving in that direction. Shielding myself from the ugliness that was going on in the world with the Kavanaugh nomination was a priority, as I didn't want to exacerbate any postpartum symptoms I was warned I might incur. Still, even then, I had no doubt that the evil fuckwad was going to get put through, even if they found a page in his calendar that had a rape installment double underlined for emphasis.

Often, trans people are excluded from certain groups because they feel we haven't experienced all of life as we are, so we have blind spots and biases incongruent with cisgender folx. We have an under-utilized perspective as far as the differences in how people are treated by presenting gender. Trans men can tell you all about how much better they're treated when they start being seen as the men they are. The worst of the fears and thoughts are a reality they're forced to realize once being "one of the guys" earns you a ticket to what men say and do when no one else is around. Trans women willingly give up the "privilege" of being seen the wrong way and have a comparative perspective that is often just as earth-shattering. For most of us, our empathy rings even more true because we've been on both sides of the equation. We were once on the inside of those conversations, seeing what people did when they thought no one else was watching, and what they say when people who don't look or act like them aren't around. Maybe that's why they want to exclude us: we know because we've seen their shit, and perhaps that's what they're afraid of.

But, as usual, the apologists' fears of being MeToo'd and their statements about how it's such a dangerous time for men are unfounded paranoia, or simply put on as a front for the continued defense of their own shitty behavior. Though I'm writing this about a few weeks in September of 2018, I can't help but look back on it knowing full well they were going to confirm this guy literally no matter what they uncovered, because when you're a rich white man in America, a different set of rules are applied to you, and there is seldom justice for those who do the most harm and never have to face most, if any, of the consequences.

It was rather peaceful to be shut off from all social media for a time, having Devyn update everyone on my progress and getting a break from the constant deluge of runny Republican shit veiled under the banner of PC Culture Being Out of Control. But there are no drugs powerful enough to both kill the pain and numb the overwhelming sense of realism that will seep through even the most protected of closed passages. While I was on week three of waiting to see if Minnesota would find in my favor in my unemployment appeal against the company that repeatedly and willfully misgendered me,

Brett Kavanaugh, who started the game on the one-yard line, complained about how his life was in tatters even though his fans had banned anyone on defense from ever touching him. Soon, he'll be bragging about how he worked harder than anyone to score that touchdown, and anyone who can't do the same must not be something something bootstraps 'Murica Jesus Freedom. Those who support this bullshit can take their Lee Greenwood, their anger over the football man not standing during the song they like, and their magnetic, symbolic patriotism and shove it. When the rules don't apply to everyone while others have to fight for months against discrimination and sometimes maybe get a pittance for it, the system is fucking broken.

While he goes to sleep, a woman's life was put on public display 26 years after Anita Hill and proved that we haven't made a damn bit of progress in that time, and he'll still find a way to consider himself the victim. Meanwhile, I had to make use of a GoFundMe just to make sure my family could pay the rent and eat during the week that Devyn stayed with me in the hospital, and many others don't even have the opportunity to make it that far in their journey.

I shed no tears, only because I no longer believe any of them will ever matter to a majority of this population, whether it's those who commit these acts or their fervent, willfully ignorant apologists. At least now that I have my vagina, they can't take it away from me no matter how hard they try. I'm only anticipating now how long it will be before other women like me are forced to travel to Thailand again because RFRA bills will make sure medical procedures they find icky are as hard to access as humanly fucking possible. I will weep for them, but not over complete lost hope in any semblance of American justice. As long as the game is rigged, they're always going to fucking win, and until I see otherwise, I'll knowingly remain a second-class citizen in my own country while white men complement their vocal fear of MeToo with continuing to harass and assault others and find a way to blame it on what she was wearing. I don't know what robes Lady Justice pulled out of the closet this time, but I'm quite sure they found a way to make sure what happened to her was her own fault.

I'm writing this as I'm recovering from the surgery, so do forgive me if I went off the rails a bit. The conflict of the peaceful time in the hospital and the helplessness I feel right now is making it very difficult to not talk about it. Yes, it was a rant, but understand that

I'm sitting on a bed mat, and I'm hardly able to move. All I have is listening to the current events on podcasts and the news, and as my first book began with the words "fuck you" about political events, it's hard to keep commentary at bay, as dated as it may be by the time you read this. I'm hoping this will both tell you the story and capture the context of the time as I was going through it. It's hard to just focus on recovery when you're constantly reminded that the system is broken.

Can't You Just Be You? Wait, Not Like That...

The #MeToo Movement was experienced by trans people as well as most of the population in a different way than even cisgender women. The following year's hashtag #WhyIDidntReport was perhaps even more difficult for the reasons that trans people are even less likely to report or risk alerting the authorities in any way. If cis women aren't taken seriously when it comes to sexual assault, trans people are a punchline.

I remember reading about campus sexual assault in the book *We Believe You*, when I found someone with whom I attended community college and had come out as a trans woman years before I did. Reaching out to her after reading her portion of the book was so important to me, and I later published her story in *Once Unspoken*. The hardest part of reading her story was just how difficult it is for trans people to report assault. It was visible that she had been assaulted in her own room, and the perpetrator laughed it off with people in the building before leaving. None of the resources at her university were willing to take it seriously, because they didn't believe a trans woman could be raped.

This wasn't in the 1980s. This was in 2013, her freshman year at Temple University, a mere cross-town trip from the University of Pennsylvania, where I was having my own freshman year in a city supposedly friendly toward us. Despite all the bragging our school officials have done about protecting trans people, the very last experience I had at the campus as a student was being followed into the bathroom and questioned by a security officer.

Trans people are barely regarded as people to a majority of the population. If we're assaulted, we'll likely be blamed for our "deviant" lifestyle, if the perpetrators of violence even know the difference between being trans and gay, which is still something most people can't differentiate. "Why can't you just be gay?" is a question many of us have been asked, so understanding the difference between identity and orientation is a long way off from a mainstream standpoint. And given the current status of the Supreme Court, not a standpoint on which we're likely to make progress anytime soon, I have no doubt we'll be banned from some kind of menial, everyday task within the next year to protect the very women they pretend to care about when it's us, but willfully disregard when it comes to women speaking up about being a survivor. They're a political tool and nothing else to a group of rich white fucks who care about nothing except getting richer and screwing over anyone who doesn't look like them.

The same goes for when we're murdered by someone who freaks out about finding out that we're trans, or who has such "panic" after having sex with us that they just have to kill us for it. Nobody cares, nobody notices, and we're misgendered by the police and media, sometimes uncorrected. So we're even less likely to report it when something happens to us, because however little law enforcement and college administrations do for cisgender women when they pretend to care about the topic, they'll do even less, if anything, for us. This includes women who have been through the surgery and have to weigh their safety against disclosing their trans status to someone who may be willing to kill them for it at any stage of the interaction. Fuck the garbage Jesus freak fratboy culture that continues to enforce this as "normal."

Oh! Be Joyful!

The first layer of dressing came off on the Sunday after the surgery (on the preceding Thursday.) This would end up being my first partial sighting of my brand new vagina. Thankfully, I couldn't see most of the stitching from the angle I had, or I'd have likely passed out even sooner. I still have a weak stomach when it comes to blood and medical stuff, so it's not hyperbolic to say so.

That's not before they had to cut the stitches that were sewn into my skin to keep the dressing on the wound. I'm pretty sure I wasn't aware that it was sewn there until I felt the first one pull away at my skin, and the pain was considerable. None of them were comfortable, but the ones toward the bottom were definitely the worst. At that point, I was absolutely not looking forward to the bolster coming out, given its coordinates and the process that would likely accompany removal.

Despite the attitude of many toward narcotics and painkillers, my doctor was more than encouraging when it came to keeping me in minimal pain. On 10mg of Oxy, which kept me mostly at a plateau between 5-7 on a scale of 10, he bumped me up to 15mg, even pushing past my initial resistance, as I knew how women were treated when it comes to pain. Also very reluctant to be on anything addicting, it came down to choosing comfort over consequences, but to have such an affirming doctor was a privilege many are not given, even after major surgeries. One woman I'm friends with was treated like a drug seeker while going through cancer treatment because she was in pain. But remember, it's a tough time to be a man right now.

Walking was slightly easier, as my overachieving ass got out of bed enough times to exhaust my partner Devyn, who deals with their own pain in the form of fibromyalgia. Already a bit restless from mostly switching between states of recline for the past few days, I knew keeping me at home was going to be a challenge. My tendencies to hike and explore to find old railroad tracks, among other things, would be a great temptation; especially with the fall colors transforming a few hours north in Duluth and along the North Shore.

I'd fallen in love with Minnesota the first time I visited in 2008, but I think it was the 2015 trip to Duluth, Two Harbors, and the Split Rock Lighthouse that sealed it for me. This place felt like home for a perpetual outsider, who grew up a Cleveland/Ohio State fan in the middle of Penn State country. The popular NFL team was determined by which one in the state was doing better at the time. When you grow up in an area that sees anyone who wasn't born there as an outsider, you never truly become one of them, but it turned out to be a consistent metaphor for being trans. Even before I was aware of that, male bonding, communication, and behavior made absolutely no sense to me. Nowadays I find the "dilly dilly" commercials as confounding as college algebra, but I'm grateful I don't have to pretend to participate anymore.

But Minnesota always felt like home. That made no sense on paper. I had no connections here outside of the internet friends I'd made thanks to writing, no family history, no job offers. I'd moved out once before in 2010, pretty much on a whim, and for a job that didn't bother to tell me it was seasonal until the day they let me go, but I was always determined to return. This was only exacerbated by coming out as transgender in 2016 amidst the election of Schmucko L'Orange, as Minnesota had local and state-level protections for transgender people, including gender identity, gender expression, and gender stereotypes. I'd guess there's a not-insignificant portion of even the LGBTQ+ community that aren't aware of those differences.

I couldn't have been happier to be there in recovery either, as I'd heard the horror stories of how those in other places had been treated, even after surgeries were performed. The very same friend from Temple I mentioned earlier was misgendered at the appointment for her orchiectomy; once again, in that supposedly affirming city of Philadelphia at a Penn Medical Center. Being affirming to trans people goes beyond acknowledging that we fucking exist. Knowing basics on how to treat us isn't an unreasonable request, especially in the medical field, and especially while representing a university with trans-inclusive healthcare.

These same thoughts flowed through my head as the anesthesiologist misgendered me moments before surgery as well.

It was far more comforting to feel at home, even though I was an hour from home, in my chosen home state. Much like my birth name and gender marker, it never felt right my entire life until I updated it appropriately. In 2017, I traveled to at least 19 states. I was happy to escape Pennsylvania and sad to return. Now? I might cancel a trip I actually want to take because I don't want to leave the state or my partners. I never understood how truly at home I felt until the first time I had to go back "home" to visit family and felt like an alien intruder. I wonder if many people feel this way, but have never left their first home in order to find out.

The first name that came to mind when I saw the swollen mounds of the upper lips of my vagina was "Oh! Be Joyful!" A reference to my Civil War nerdery, an alcoholic concoction with a celebratory name seemed relevant enough for finally feeling right in my own body. However, I wasn't prepared for the overwhelming satisfaction I'd experience for this very reason.

Everything not only matched up, but it was an unbelievable sensation. Not seeing any part of the unfortunate appendage I'd been born with when looking down was downright addicting. Even through the screams of the stitches being snipped out, I internally recognized it as one step closer to everything being a status quo that I could live with. Now, as the poor swollen girl was three days past surgery and partially revealed to me, it was beyond having no regrets. It was peace; a peace I'd never wholly felt until that moment, and one I didn't know I was missing until the underwear area matched up with the rest of me.

It was…

Correct.

Oppressively Hopelessly Romantic

Throughout Sunday, my restlessness started to get to me. It wasn't quite being quelled by getting up to walk multiple times a day, and despite my best attempts, I couldn't completely avoid wanting to create material. All things considered, I did a pretty good job of resting and not working, but I think for the sake of being grateful for my partners, it was a reasonable exception.

I wrote a free verse piece for each of them to express my gratitude as they dealt with me in recovery. I'll share each of them here. Each of them were done on a phone through Google Docs, so while I was mostly steering clear of social media, I wasn't completely disconnected from the world. There were a lot of painkillers and my mind was cloudy, but letting the people I love know that I appreciated everything they did to me was beyond important. I've never been good at accepting help or allowing others to do things for me, so I showed said appreciation in the only way I really could while mostly remaining in a hospital bed.

Aiden

You are my beautiful boy, the very light of my day and the safety throughout the night. Our steps lock in sync, and our journeys can never be without each other.

The years have felt like generations, yet the passions only fan deeper flames that grow by the second. Life without you isn't worth remembering, because anything before you isn't relevant to who I am. You're my rock, my foundation, my very essence of being.

I cannot ascribe enough of the dictionary for your smile alone, as it guides me through any darkness I could ever fathom. Your gliding touch and your hand's grasp are more essential to me than blood in my veins.

Nothing I could ever hope to achieve in life is more valuable than knowing I managed to be worthy of the love of your heart. The most beautiful soul I've ever encountered who sees the very best in anyone he can radiates pure goodness and goodwill; our legal last names are solely perfect for it because you enrich the lives of anyone lucky enough to even hear your laugh by chance proximity.

Aiden, life's perfection is every second anything is fortunate enough to exist near you. My heart only beats in responsive nature to your direction, and no matter how many people I love, nothing has ever even slightly dampened the very bloodsource from which I desperately needed to marry you. I'm the most fortunate person alive for being the one who gets to say she's your wife, because nothing of which I could ever dream or fantasize does even a day of your existence justice.

Devyn

Through distance, words were kept in the context of a fling that was never to be my intention. No fly by night or jovial hookup was ever on my agenda when it came to you. My heart was toast the second my breath was stolen by your gaze.

Our lives have permanently intersected and joined together, forging our paths to follow the same permanent highs regardless of the time of day or levels of energy that sometimes impede our incessant needs for affection.

Your voice soothes my very soul, especially when it's taking words off a page and transforming them into a movie on the back of my eyelids where all parts are played by you. You narrate my entire life, because no words have ever left your mouth that made me question how you feel about me, nor I you. Our story is almost boring in a way because it never developed any conflict whatsoever. "Hey, what a beautiful weekend. Move in? Kay. You're family from now on."

No words or actions I could ever take or create do this love justice. I feel woefully inept in the contribution I've made, only because I'm still left in amazement every time your amazing story ends with picking me after being around the world. I'm forever indebted to whatever programming the world provided that made me the ideal selection, because lightning somehow struck and I caught it in a bottle that Eli likely threw aside by accident. A silly podcast about dick jokes is what made me fall in love with you.

As I recover and still find ways to be amazed that you really are here to help me every step of the way, my only hope is to continue to make you proud and do all I can possibly manage to produce. Every word I put out for the world's consumption is also narrated by you, because without your voice being the pinnacle of my existence, nothing I made would ever have come out the way it did.

Isaac

How does one accurately describe their love for someone when they've already managed to survive a catastrophe of epic proportions? What words can be written that sum up the idea of overcoming mass manipulation of circumstances? What can one add to the tremendous graph of emotions ranging from the lowest in years to the triumphant victorious high of a defeated nemesis?

What I know is our journey circumnavigated disaster, leading to points where only the hope for a peaceful resolution someday remained, where I'd have to call her your wife and know I'd always be a distant second at best if I hoped to remain at all.

I watched as I predicted the actions she would take, yet unable to stop her tenacious sociopathic destruction, poisoning our love like a virus hellbent on surviving via the tears of the broken-hearted.

Yet, I would've kept to my word to not ever criticizing her to keep you in my life if I had to, because waking up and seeing your morning messages became such an integral part of my day that I was void of routine from the start and thus plagued to the perfection of assertion.

I would've watched you marry her if it meant I even occasionally got to chat you up about trains and fashion choices, with everything else off limits and knowing that a smug smirk was following every tangentially inept construction of sentences to live within that confinement.

Trading away the depth to which our uniquely intimate relationship of distance and unforeseen connection for the simple privilege of retaining occasionally hearing your voice saying anything at all was always worth it, because the alternative of not having you at all would've rendered me a permanent stain of regret upon the gallery of the map of hearts.

However, surviving and conquering the foe of truth, love, and genuine empathy leaves me free to compel my innermost joyfulness, something I kept stored away for fear that it would never again meet its equal exchange.

The thread of words with which you weave through my soul, unique even with it's equally respected counterparts, has become so essential to maintaining my very essence of being that I now can't imagine having to compromise it away, even though I was willing to because you are and will always be worth whatever it takes, even if it's living the lie that would've been never being able to proclaim my undying love and affection for you.

Our magical train has returned to its rightful tracks, and every trek we make toward another glamorous sunset by the lakes to hear the call of the loons only receives more soulful gratuity, for meeting its polar opposite and overcoming its willful sabotage has made every single moment of the lilt in your accent and the glint in your eyes worth the extra momentary glance of observant serenity.

My Isaac, my shining masculine beacon of pure, motivated love and compassion, I live for making you proud and causing those brilliant moments of surprised expression that decorate your face of fading scars and suppressed fear. For if I can help you believe that at least in one place, you will never lack of love, family, and hope again, I consider it superior to any accomplishment in the external world I could've ever fathomed.

Stay with me, sweet boy. Love others as you need, and take all the space for regeneration and solitude you require, for any moment I'm lucky enough to share with you will always be more than any dream could hope to substitute. You are a dream, Isaac; for you carry my heart and drive to succeed along with your every gesture and helpful thought. Nothing I ever write will be able to match the moment we gaze into each other's eyes and know everything we've left unsaid remains the purest truth we've always dreamed of but woefully fell short with those not worthy of that intimacy.

My rebirth upon this year comes with ours, and may you never know another day that retracts from what we've saved from disaster.

These pieces may not have much to do with the overall arc of this story, but without the three of them, I don't know if I'd have been the quiet, well-behaved patient I ended up being. Keeping me comfortable, calm, and safe from overdoing it, even from a distance, my partners contributed more to my recovery than running errands and staying with me in the hospital. Without the support and love from my husband, I may never have come out in the first place. Thus, I wouldn't have even met the other two, let alone everything else that transpired since I yelled "fuck you!" in a hate pastor's face. I owe them my life, and I do not say that hyperbolically, as I truly don't know if I would've survived another year in the closet. Every "sir" was a dagger. Every "he" was a punch to the face. Every time my parents and family called me by a name I didn't associate with myself, it pushed me down further into a well of depression, and even the strongest among us can only survive so many wounds.

I don't know how long it would've taken without them, but I do know one day longer than it was would've been too long. Actually, at the point I did come out, it had already been years too long, so I'm glad I skipped class that October Monday and had my phone out for video proof. So many events can be traced back to a happenstance in one's life, but without Aiden making sure I was still loved as I hid in the closet, dealt with the trauma of a rape, and came to terms with who I truly was, even while hiding it, none of it would've happened without him.

Medically-Prescribed Glass Dildos

Day Five. Tuesday. I woke up with a massive migraine and tension headache at the same time. Not exactly the most pleasant circumstances under which to realize that the room is going to be packed and you're going to have very painful items removed from your body.

I begged the nurse for some ibuprofen, because none of the painkillers were for headaches. All the blinds were drawn, I had a pillow over my face, and I was laying as flat as possible trying to tune out the world. Sure enough, the medical posse wanders in, and given how busy they are on a day-to-day basis, headaches were not going to hold them back.

The metal bar above my head, which until then I assumed was for getting off the bed, doing pull-ups Rocky-style, and banging your head into when you're tall, was now going to get a new purpose: the hospital bed equivalent of the "Oh Shit! Handle." If you're not familiar with that term, those are the handles above the window in the car that people tend to grab onto when they're nervous or scared, especially if they panic and say "oh shit!" Thus the name, albeit I'm sure I yelled words much harsher than those two.

First coming were some more snips; the rest of the dressing and the bolster, which I'll remind you is a condom filled with gauze literally sewn into my five-day-old vagina; the bottom opening of which is freshly stitched. Every snip was like getting stabbed in the gut with a knitting needle, or if you're a cis dude, it's like when you're pulling on something really strenuously, your hand slips, and you punch yourself in the dick. Except a bunch of times, because there was more than one stitch. I don't know how many there were, because I was screaming for every single one of them while also having two different blinding headaches.

Then, the wound drain was next. This was a tube above my pubic area, right next to a bruise that looked like I tried to vault over a fence and hit the bar across my hips. The nurses had been constantly impressed that it didn't need to be emptied very much, and I assumed that was good news. I'd accidentally pulled on it the previous night while trying to sleep though, and I should've learned my lesson from that moment of nearly biting my tongue off with my breath held. Getting a tube pulled out of my skin near a bruise that huge in an inconvenient place was like having a splinter and trying to get it out with a splintered pair of wooden tweezers. The other denizens of the hospital heard my audition to become the new backup singer of Against Me!, but likely didn't get the reference so they opted for hypothesizing that someone was in pain instead. They were also correct.

Last but certainly not least, the catheter. If I can say one nice thing about that urethra-plaguing nightmare, it was the first and only time in my life I didn't have to wake up multiple times a night to pee, cause that shit was *covered*. What a relief. That's also like swan-diving off the Hennepin County Bridge but appreciating the quality of the Instagram photo you got on the way down. #regrets #seemedlikeagoodideaatthetime.

So there I was; pulling myself toward the ceiling while letting Fred Flintstone know it was time for the end of his shift, and a catheter was being pulled out of my urethra in the middle of my five-day-old vagina, which had recently been tenderized by the removal of the bolster and stitches that held it there moments earlier. I'm not sure if I told the doctor performing these actions that his mother had taken upon herself some extracurricular matronly duties, but I can't deny that I may have alluded to his mother as an unseemly woman of the night. If my internal monologue matched the syllables escaping my mouth at terminal velocity, I'd like to take this opportunity to apologize to him, the team, the residents of the sixth floor of the Eisenberg Center, and… just in case… Jesus, because his picture was in my room at one point in time.

But wait, there's more!

The doctor then proceeds to hand me a mirror and a white bag. Inside the bag were three lawn dart-sized, smooth glass dildos that were going to be spending a lot of time with me for a while. Four half-hour sessions a day for the first three weeks to be exact; before I progressed to the bigger size, and eventually Big Bertha, who would let me know just how much everyone else would be lying in the future if any of my potential partners were phallically-inclined. The mirror? So I could see him putting a dilator inside my vagina in all its black-stitched glory while enough people to form a hospital Lynyrd Skynyrd tribute band watched on. Insert it pointing toward my back after plenty of lube, and it was the kind that could create a good *Home Alone* pratfall... so that was reassuring... and once you feel it hit the back, hold it there with gentle pressure.

You know how on the first day at the job, they want you to simulate a customer service interaction while other people watch and judge your performance? It was like that, except gently fucking myself with a tube that could have lights wrapped around it and be used to direct airplanes to their gates. So, you know, minimally awkward. Finally, they all left, and the nurse who I thought I'd annoyed came back and not only took care of me, but let me know I'd been the least difficult patient following this kind of surgery they'd ever had. I'd be able to take that in after the headaches receded into the night like the former olives to my now-inverted martini. Good times had by all.

They'd given me the option to go home that day, but after that several minute catastrophe of invading-solitude proportions combined with the feeling of staring at some dude who got his brand new LED headlights and wants to show them off while driving toward you at 2am, all I wanted was ibuprofen and sleep.

I woke up several hours later, with the headache finally receding into the distance like the ships of Columbus in the good timeline, and while I still felt like I'd banged my head into a disco ball made out of a lava lamp, the choice to go home held one particularly motivating factor in its favor: my cute, loving, unbelievably amazing husband, and being able to sleep next to him instead of reminding people what my birthday was at four in the morning made an awful good case for itself.

Enough of one that I decided, despite my headspace... Yes, I want to go home. I want to be with my Aiden. Nothing in the world would have sounded better in that moment.

Rumble Strips Give Me PTSD

Riding in a car is difficult when you can't sit down.

I counted on the need for cushion and support, but I also had no basis for comparison. I'd either been in the bed or walking around for the previous five days, so I hadn't eve attempted to sit yet. The neck pillow Devyn got me would have to suffice as a seat donut in the car. Already being six feet tall, this was going to make not bumping my head on the ceiling even more of a pain. I was surprised that the hospital crew didn't make me ride down in a wheelchair, as that was something I'd always been told about being hospitalized.

My friend Bridget was picking us up, but wasn't at the pickup area when we got there. Not expecting standing after five minutes of walking to be this hard, I texted urgently for her to find us. Already breathing heavily but unable to sit on the curb for obvious reasons, every second of being on my feet became more agonizing.

She eventually found her way around the building to where we were, and I had to fight my instinct to put all the bags in the car. Not lifting anything over ten pounds for a few months needed to override the innate need to grab everything myself and lift all the heavy items. With Devyn having fibromyalgia, the roles were reversed for the first time in our relationship, and that would take some getting used to.

I think I was in the car for maybe 10 of the 75 minutes of the drive before I re-positioned myself on my back with my knees in the air. Every bump felt like I was landing crotch-first on a balance beam, so the motion sickness of looking out the window from the side while laying down was unfortunately preferable. I've never been in such ardent favor of improving infrastructure than being in the backseat on route 52, hoping that no potholes would unexpectedly meet Bridget's tires. They did.

If getting in the car was a long, painful process, getting out and then up the stairs to my room was going to be a real adventure. It's five steps up to the door, and then a flight of stairs up to my room. Many of my friends suggested staying on the couch in our living room for a time, but with two affectionate and needy cats, kids who don't understand the concept of turning the lights off, and the need to sleep most of the day, our bedroom was the only option. At the very back of the second floor, with its wood paneling that made it preferable for my podcasting equipment, even the slight step up to the door was going to be a bit tricky for a time. I'd only walked on even floors while in the hospital. Weight limits and pressure were easier to avoid that way.

Getting up the steps was somewhere between crawling around blackout drunk trying to find the bed and being paranoid that Grandma's going to fall when you're helping her find her keys. Even breathing wrong had its painful effects at five days into recovery, so one step at a time was its own nightmare of consequences. I didn't plan on spending much time going back downstairs if I could help it.

My sweet husband Aiden managed to have the room picture perfect by the time I got there, and I only knew how much my heart was aching from missing him once I saw his hopeful but terrified expression. Once again swallowing my pride, I allowed them to help me take my clothes off as I got into bed. Sleeping on my side was still an impossibility, so I'd be spending more time on my back than I ever had in my life. It was worse being at home in that aspect, because I didn't have the buttons to elevate my upper half to ease the pressure or pain like I did in the hospital bed.

There are needs for recovery for this kind of surgery you don't consider. Mostly because even the published literature on this topic is utter garbage. A *Washington Post* article dated 2015 - a liberal newspaper and when Obama was president - discussed the procedure while misgendering the shit out of trans people the entire time and referring to celebrities by their deadnames. "FTM is more difficult and expensive, which is why fewer women choose to have surgery on their genitals. Men retain their prostates."[1] If you can't even bother to gender correctly a trans woman who has gotten through the process of a vaginoplasty, you don't know the first thing about trans people; equally as true when you refer to trans men by saying that *women* don't choose to have it as often. Run your shit article by at least one trans person, for fuck's sake. This wasn't 1975, where the only frame of reference most people had was *The Rocky Horror Picture Show*. Talk to, I don't know, one trans person before you exploit and minimize our experience to

---

[1]https://www.washingtonpost.com/news/to-your-health/wp/2015/02/09/heres-how-sex-reassignment-surgery-works/?utm_term=.de7d39b2ad72&noredirect=on

our genitals by writing about the topic you're clearly covering for the "wow" factor from those who haven't dealt with this their whole lives. We don't go through surgery to begin our transition. The surgery is usually either the end or close to the end of it. Even I, who was only on hormones for 26 months before having surgery, lived openly as a woman for that long, and far more years in the closet.

This only reinforces the notion that Julia Serano discussed in her book *Whipping Girl*: "If cissexual academics truly believe that transsexual and intersex people can add new perspectives to existing dialogues about gender, then they should stop reinterpreting our experiences and instead support transsexual and intersex intellectual endeavors and works of art. Instead of exploiting our experiences to further their own careers, they should insist that their universities make a point of hiring transsexual and intersex faculty, and that their publishers put out books by gender-variant writers. And they should finally acknowledge the fact that they have no legitimate claim to use transsexual and intersex identities, struggles, and histories for their own purposes."[2] Or, to put it another way, stop being on the outside looking in to our experiences as if we were a reality show weight loss transition. How many trans stories are told by the non-LGBTQ media where the before and after pictures are the focus? Not only does it put the onus on trans people to "pass" so that they can be pretty or handsome enough to be gendered correctly, but it treats us as a scientific circus project designed to entertain the curiosities of those who will go back to pretending we

---

[2]Serano, Julia. *Whipping Girl: A Transsexual Woman on Sexism and the Scapegoating of Femininity*

don't exist the minute they finish an article. And we wonder why a majority of people think gender is strictly determined by genitals...

I didn't go through the vaginoplasty to "become" a woman. I went through it because it was the final affirming piece to the woman I already am. Exploiting the trans experience and reducing us to our genitals or surgeries dehumanizes us on a level only matched by those who would see us harmed for daring to not disclose our trans status to a potential date. Or kick us out of a bathroom. Or deny us medical care. We don't exist so that curious cisgender people can peer in on one aspect of our lives and then only look at us when they want to sneak in their taboo porn preference while simultaneously calling us men, shemales, ladyboys, disgusting, perverted, against nature, trannies, traps, he-shes, or any of the other entries on our antagonizers' Google search history. We're people. Trans women, trans men, enbies, and anyone else on the gender spectrum; we are people trying to live our lives as comfortably as possible, not a curiosity-quenching thought experiment to discuss with your bodies in the drunk tank. Stop publishing trite and inaccurate bullshit like this. You're not fucking helping.

Among the needs one may not think of before they're necessary: bed and underwear pads. A lot of blood and discharge is leaving the wound area nearly all the time, and it'll ruin your bed if you don't have something beneath it. Sleeping with a pad on has its own difficulties, so having pads to put on the bed at least made the experience of sleeping without any underwear possible.

Using three dilators for months at a time is going to require a lot of lubricant. Short of finding the source of the drums of lube spoken about in *Cards Against Humanity* or sent to the Y'all-Queda domestic terrorist hangout in Oregon a couple years ago. Wait, they got pardoned, so they were only exercising their free speech as white men while black people get murdered in their own home and somehow still get blamed for it, my bad. Four times a day, I was getting well acquainted with my phallus-shaped vagina saver, and I wasn't about to shortchange the amount of lube I would be using to add depth to the chamber of science penetration. Sure, I ended up feeling like a Slip-N-Slide at the Playboy Mansion, but that would all be taken care of by the douche I had to put there twice a day.

And by douche, I am not referring to my ex-girlfriend. Especially the one who told people she was living in a cult while I had her under my roof. At least not this time.

There's nothing more exciting than pulling out the dilator for the fourth time that day, and then going to sit spread eagle on the toilet, which at this point is still incredibly difficult to do at all, while your partner finds the right place for the canal entrance with a white Old Faithful stick of salt water in order to make sure you don't have a crotch funk resembling the eggs you forgot to put in the refrigerator last week.

Well, maybe there's *one* thing more exciting than that.

Some friends arrived bearing gifts. Gifts of a certain painkilling persuasion that doesn't involve swallowing, if you catch my drift. Allegedly. While the door was open and everyone was having a "Rissy's home safely with a vagina in tow" love discussion, one of our cats decided to use my crotch as a crash pad. Needless to say, my neighbors probably either think I died or was just listening to an Arnold movie really loudly. Or maybe one with the other, who knows?

And why would you need underwear pads? Imagine how many I had to go through while blood was escaping the wounds both internally and externally with all the usual marks of healing at the most sensitive position on your body that you can't help but move because you're a person who exists and not a statue in the park. I went through several in the first day, because I would quickly feel like a toddler with a wet diaper, but I was banned from doing anything to aid myself in the process. My partners became my changing team, whether it was refilling my water flagon or changing the pad because I failed Pull-Ups school.

One more item you're going to need that you may not have considered? Stool softeners.

The anesthesia alone makes it difficult to get things moving in the chambers of Congress within you. Add in the painkillers and lack of mobility, and pretty soon you're more full of shit than an anti-vaxxer at a Goop parade. The number of stool softeners I swallowed was rivaled only by the bowls of cereal I was consuming in order to blast a fire in the hole (the other one) to get the system working again. Unfortunately, there was a work stoppage that continued through day five, so the best I could hope for was an event that would be the equivalent of all the RFRA laws passed by the non-internal Chambers of Congress to make sure

Christians have the legal right to discriminate against anyone or anything they find icky, 'cause freedumb. At least mine wouldn't affect anyone except whomever had the unlucky fortune to use the bathroom after I did.

But, alas, I was home. I was in pain, somewhat miserable, constantly feeling dirty, unable to sit on the toilet without holding myself up, and going through the archives of the *New York Times* crossword puzzles like they'd be deleted the next day, but I was home. That, at the very least, made the recovery a little better. Well, that and the non-swallowed painkilling sustenance graciously provided to us by people who allegedly delivered them to suit our hour of need. If I was going to be mostly immobile for the next few weeks, at least I could make my music awesome in the process.

The Handmaid's Tale Isn't a How-to Manual

I'd love to write more about the process of discovering

myself and all the happy things that have come with it,

but sometimes that's impossible.

I've made no attempt to hide my disdain for current events while I reflect on the recent past, but this is an issue so extreme and personal that I need to address it right now as I have first taken in the information. I wrote in this piece earlier that I was in a race to the vagina against Trump, and while some may accuse me of hyperbole, I awoke this morning to an article from the *New York Times* where Trump is literally trying to make us illegal.

He wasn't even inaugurated yet when people were telling me to calm down and give him a chance. We weren't supposed to worry when the White House LGBT page disappeared on the first day. The military ban was only to appease the evangelicals. The RFRA protections to make sure medical personnel who discriminate against us are kept safe were only protecting the First Amendment. Banning the CDC from using the word "transgender" was only a harmless decree.

The headline today is: "Trump Administration Eyes Defining Transgender Out of Existence." Y'all wanna be fucking allies? Now's the time! "The department argued in its memo that key government agencies needed to adopt an explicit and uniform definition of gender as determined 'on a biological basis that is clear, grounded in science, objective and administrable.'"[3]

3

https://www.nytimes.com/2018/10/21/us/politics/transgender-trump-administration-sex-definition.html?action=click&module=Top+Stories&pgtype=Homepage&fbclid=IwAR1IiPzJcDRz

Am I allowed to be pissed off yet, or will the shitty centrists and apologists find a way to rationalize this one too?

The TERFs love to hold signs that say "Biology Not Bigotry" while simultaneously endorsing bigotry of this kind by allying with the far right against us. As if the alt-right won't turn on them the second they get what they want in regard to us. I guess the cis lesbians who find common ground with evangelicals don't realize they're against their existence too. If I've learned anything from the last two years, it's that the steps the administration takes are not cloaked anymore, and they never stop. There is no "too far." The science doesn't matter to them because they've never actually read any of it. It's not like I was able to get surgery because there's no

---

1m_xOYZalyF51-N6fTiUsUldJ0ZZfyXRn3swJh3Q4WHP3W
o

science on transgender people. The science is there; they're not fucking interested. If they were, they wouldn't be climate deniers, but that's another topic for another book.

Science is just another buzzword thrown out to thinly veil their attempts to subjugate anyone who doesn't look like they do or pray to the right god. They don't know science any more than they care about bathroom statistics when it comes to protecting women and children, but they'll appoint someone credibly accused of sexual assault to the Supreme Court because, you know, they care so much about women. None of these are isolated incidents, and this agenda from the administration and anti-trans activists was not hidden.

Everyone who claims the 2016 election was about economic hardships of lower and middle class white people are only hiding their own motivations to have their class and religion put above the rest in all social consideration. If you accepted bigotry and racism as part of a campaign that also had economic benefits, you're still a bigot and a racist. Just because you didn't vote for this for that reason; that isn't an excuse. You were still willing to either accept it or look past it, and silence is complicity. We've been telling you our lives are in danger, and you've been telling us to calm down and that it'll all be all right.

It's not alright. This is less than a month before the midterm elections, and that is not a coincidence. The bathroom fear was used by the right to drive paranoid bigots to the polls, and this is the same worm attached to a fishing hook of shittiness.

Don't take the fucking bait.

You know that Holocaust poem by Martin Niemolller that conservatives graciously misquoted when Obama was president, about who they first came for?

"First they came for the socialists, and I did not speak out—because I was not a socialist.

Then they came for the trade unionists, and I did not speak out—because I was not a trade unionist.

Then they came for the Jews, and I did not speak out—because I was not a Jew.

Then they came for me—and there was no one left to speak for me."
4

Well, it certainly wasn't us, but it's relevant here. They're keeping immigrant children in detention camps and banned people from certain Muslim countries from traveling here, but they're mostly brown, so your

---

4

https://encyclopedia.ushmm.org/content/en/article/martin-nie moeller-first-they-came-for-the-socialists faux-morally superior complex made sure to spout buzzwords like "terrorism" and "legal immigration." And, if you think they'll stop at us, you never read the end of the poem. If you're not a cis, straight, Christian, rich white man, they're coming for you next. I expect *Roe v. Wade* to be overturned in less than a year. Elections have fucking consequences, and while we can all get an easy laugh out of misquoting Elizabeth Warren about her DNA test, none of this shit would be happening right now if she or Hillary Clinton or Bernie Sanders or pretty much anyone without an R next to their name were in charge right now.

If you still support this administration, you do not deserve forgiveness. I don't care how many people won't date you.[5] There are social consequences for supporting bigoted, racist theocrats, and you deserve every last one of them. Turn off FOX News and talk to a person you don't already know for once. If we truly believe in the idea of America as a place for freedom and prosperity, we cannot also accept the idea that certain kinds of people deserve to be kept in prison camps, banned from traveling to the country, or legislated out of existence. It's more than saying you support the troops and blowing shit up on the Fourth of July. I don't care how many yellow ribbons or Wounded Warrior magnets you have. The hypocrisy of Americans talking about freedom on a foundation of genocide and slavery is bad enough, but we have unprecedented access to information that gives us

---

5

https://www.businessinsider.com/trump-staffers-are-complai
n-that-they-cant-date-in-dc-2018-6

the ability to be better in the present and future. Do better. And do it before it's too little, too late. For those who have already died because you just weren't comfortable with Hillary Clinton, it already is.

A Letter to the Prime Minister of a Place That Thinks We're Actually People

Honorable Prime Minister,

I doubt this message finds you in surprise, and I doubt I'm the only one who has written you in this regard. I'm a transgender American woman with a trans husband and a non-binary partner. We live in Minnesota, about five hours away from Canada, and part of the reason we moved here was to be close... just in case something like what's happening did.

We realize how we're portrayed across the world, and those who fall in line with our President's policies and vision for what the world should be deserve it, but a lot of us are terrified right now. Whereas your country includes us in legal protections, we wake up to news that the President is trying to legislate us out of existence.

I can't speak to what my government has done in the last two years. A lot of us have tried to do what we could, and you'll see in my signature the receipts from that, but we can't risk being arrested because we'll be sent to the wrong prison and be in more danger than we already are. With a party's heist of the Supreme Court and the lower courts as well, combined with this administration's ability to do literally anything and get away with it, we don't know what more to do. We screamed when the White House LGBT page was removed, when he banned us from the military, from the CDC mentioning us, from workplace discrimination protection, and making sure religious medical workers had a safe haven to discriminate against us, so I doubt literally trying to make us illegal is going to be any different in terms of the apathy of our supposed allies in the community. Oh, and they're doing all they can to keep us from getting passports too, so even if we wanted to come there, we'd likely be denied the ability to do so.

I know we're not your concern, and America is certainly due the consequences of its decisions. But there are communities down here that are terrified, and have been so as we've seen what they've done to Muslim travelers and asylum seekers to the south. We're afraid many would see it as poetic justice if we tried to do the same to escape a tyrannical criminal and were put in camps too, but we know that's not how Canada does things. We're envious.

What do we do, as American Citizens, Mr. Prime Minister? Our family is literally prepared to make a break for it any day, even in a state where we're protected, because the new policies will likely roll all of that back. We don't know what to do, and we don't know if we'll even be able to get there if it gets any worse, and judging from the article in the Times today, it's going to. They've rigged the game against us and made it as difficult as possible to escape. Help!

Sincerely,

Marissa Alexa McCool

Graduate Student, Wife, Mother, and Frightened American

I Think It's Falling Off. This Is How It Ends!

AUTHOR'S NOTE: I realize that my writing may seem harshly political if you're not at all familiar with me. However, part of the point of this piece is to describe what it's like to exist as a trans person, and unfortunately, we can't only talk about the past. Even in the short time since I've gotten surgery (38 days as of this writing), enough has changed that I've had to address just in that amount of time. To only talk about the recovery and not what was going on in the world during it would be a disservice. But I'm back to the main topic here, at least until and unless something else happens. (It will.)

The first week of recovery was a lot harder than the five days in the hospital. For one, I didn't have nurses coming to check on me every two hours, nor someone in the next room playing the TV at a volume normally reserved for the IMAX screening of the next *Avengers* movie. The problem though is that our nextdoor neighbors are the loudest people on the planet, and short of finding a way to soundproof the house, it's impossible to tune out their car alarms, motorboat engine tests, and drunken deck construction. Being able to keep it dark and quiet for the most part sure was nice. I was able to sleep at times not normally designated for it because time was pretty much irrelevant.

I hope I never have to have a catheter again, but it sure was easier than trying to pee with a new vagina. I didn't realize it at the time, but the lips were still sewn together. That was a relief to figure out later, as I thought I was just really bad at using the new urethra. I don't know if it was due to the medicine or still lingering effects from spironolactone, but I had to pee a ridiculous amount, especially at night. Sitting down was still something of an issue, so I probably ignored my weight-lifting limit by constantly having to hold myself up and pee at the same time.

Sleeping was the hardest, though. I didn't have a reclining bed, so just laying back and going to sleep wasn't a possibility for that reason as well. Also, I'm a side sleeper: I tend to turn to one side, snuggle my Berry Bear, and put a pillow between my knees with them bent at a 90 degree angle. Attempting this in the hospital would only get me off my back for two or three minutes, even with a pillow fort between my knees. Most times, I'd find myself on my back with my legs split like a catcher, which I wasn't supposed to do, but I couldn't lay flat for very long either, as it would put too much pressure on OBJ.

The pain was decreasing, but it would get worse at night. The second night we were home, Carla went to the bathroom in the middle of the night and told Devyn that her vagina was going to fall off. I'm guessing this feeling came from a sensation that was like combining a lot of BenGay with a really bad brush burn. The entire stitched area seemed like it was being cut by a laser when I laid on my back for too long, but there wasn't much I could do about that, as described.

Also keeping me awake were the wet pads, whether they were in my underwear or on my bed. I was still leaking a lot of blood and discharge, and trying to lay back down on cold liquid wasn't conducive to rest. This was likely at least partially exacerbated at night from all the lube I was using to make sure OBJ was appropriately dilated. Christ, I was gently fucking myself for two hours a day at that point.

One night during the first week, I was in so much pain because, in addition to the aforementioned laser burns, the upper lift on the left side split the stitching about a half inch, and the skin in between was turning black. Anything that brushed against it hurt, including my own legs when I laid down, which also made the need for spread legs more pressing.

Having never had surgery before, I wasn't sure what the expectations were to be; as far as pain management, blood, discharge, stitching, or even bowel movements. By the third day home, I was eating fiber-rich cereal, taking a stool softener every four hours, and drinking as much water every second that I could. I both wanted to make sure things would get moving and that my stomach wouldn't resemble the current administration; though being that full of shit would be an impressive feat. I probably bothered the nurses through the Mayo app more times than I care to count, and a few of them involved sending them pictures of the area of concern. It figures that my first vag pics were solicited for medical reasons.

Dilating didn't really hurt, so that was something of a relief. Putting the douche stick in had unfortunate consequences if Devyn missed, however. Having not previously had a vagina, and most of it still being brand new, I couldn't quite tell when something was inside the canal or not, but I did find out several times what pushing in the wrong place would do.

I finally had a BM at eight days. It wasn't much, but it was relieving to turn those stomach gurgles into something productive. Unfortunately, the next few days were filled with so much time on the porcelain that my skin became sensitive to even wet wipes and the bidet, let alone toilet paper.

There was one more circumstance I wasn't counting on though, and this was the biggest surprise of them all. My libido was out of goddamn control.

Many trans women say it takes them a year to regain any kind of sensation, and sometimes they don't at all. Yet, during my first week at home, I was doing all I could to not grind up against my partners. Even with the weird phenomenon of Phantom Boners, the urge to get release was there, especially as I felt correct in my body. I didn't have to close my eyes and pretend when touching myself anymore, though I was likely still banned from any kind of activity for quite a while. But, when you're sexually active at a young age and have a relatively easy time getting laid for nearly twenty years, a cold turkey stoppage has its effects.

And it sure didn't take long for my libido to be over this recovery shit and ready for the action it was made for. Alas, I couldn't even lay anywhere but my back, so bloodied, in pain, and gross must've been the least attractive I ever felt while also feeling whole as a body. What a weird mindspace to be; in pain, gross, but horny as hell.

It really is puberty all over again.

Slow Down and Rest? But There's Fuckery Afoot!

I've always been one to take on all I can handle, especially since coming out. I've worked on as many as six podcasts at one time, not to mention my attendance at Penn was four years of a 100-mile daily commute four times a week. Slowing down and resting is not something I've ever been able to do.

You may have noticed that earlier in this piece, I've referred to events that were current at the time of their writing, and that was with my effort to not be doing schoolwork, podcasting, or participating in anything strenuous. I don't know how to not do anything, but I got a crash course in not being *able* to do anything in the weeks following surgery prior to my school and podcast comebacks (for which I allowed myself the absolute minimum allotted recovery time of four weeks because that's who I am as a person.)

Among my other routines and activities, I made an active effort to get in ten thousand steps a day whenever possible. Most of these steps would be walked in a nearby park called Kaposia Landing, as it contained several of my favorite outdoor Rissy happy triggers: eagles, water, trains, and bridges. The main loop around Kaposia is about 1.8 miles, and I would regularly walk it twice at one time, and I'd also visit twice on nice days.

After a week of recovery, plus the five days in the hospital, I was desperate to see something pretty. Fresh air, feeling the sun, moving around; these all sounded like healthy needs for a recovery process. Once I finally was antsy enough, I struggled to get in the car while using a pillow, and did my best to get us the ¾ of a mile to the park. The first time was the wakeup call in terms of my body catching up, as I made it *maybe* a few hundred feet before I started hurting. Aiden allowed me to hold his shoulder as I limped along the sidewalk, but even then, it wasn't enough. I'd also made the mistake of parking at Simon's Ravine, which involved walking over a bridge with an incline on each side, and I was wiped out shortly after crossing into the park.

Stubborn as all hell, I managed to stumble my way to a park bench so I could see the Swing Bridge, which is an active railroad bridge over the Mississippi River near the park. My fatigue and pain, however, weren't aided by sitting down, so it was a no-win solution. And, for how tired I may have been trying to get back to the car, that was nothing compared to the effort it took to get back up to my safe haven in the corner of the second floor. Each step outside took all the strength I thought I had, and I gave out about halfway up the inside stairway. Aiden did his best to pull me the rest of the way up while encouraging me and being as patient as a man can be expected. I collapsed on the bed when we finally got there, and both Aiden and Devyn had to take my shoes and clothes off, help me get into bed, and worry as I fell asleep almost immediately. My spirit of initiative had met its ultimate match: a body going through recovery.

At that point, Devyn lent/forced me to use their walker next time I had to go anywhere, and after hitting that wall so shortly after feeling energetic, I, for once, wasn't arguing. I'd end up needing it at my two-week post-op appointment, which became its own adventure, but at least it was an easier way to both visit the park and not be a complete mess by the time I got back.

The little patch of black had become unbearable, and my gait had changed to avoid rubbing my left lip, which might have made me a contender for Monty Python's Ministry for Silly Walks, but it wasn't pleasant.

Walking that way and sleeping with my legs in a position that would at least be more desirable once I healed, I begged the doctor for answers. In addition, I had a patch of white near the bottom on the same side that looked like it had either chafed or died. This was of multiple concerns, as I couldn't avoid it at all since I had to dilate four times a day. I noticed I could move it with a wet wipe, but it was still attached, so I was terrified to do anything. I imagined the nurses checking the email were expecting my repeated questions and concerns at that point, but when a recovery manual tells you to take any number of listed concerns to your doctor's attention, you do what that manual says, especially when you have no basis of recovery comparison.

My friends Maddy, Hertzey, and Bridget really stepped up here too. For several weeks, they made sure we had dinners to eat, and they transported my daughter to school, since the bus route didn't come there (though strangely enough, my son's did, and the school was less than a mile away.) The GoFundMe didn't make its projected goal, but it got close, and that's way more than a lot of fundraisers in similar situations are able to achieve. I truly hope I'm able to pay that forward someday.

Oh You Better Believe I Can Fuck

It's been three months since I got my vagina. Outside of some small discharge that I still get in my underwear, I'm pretty much healed. The scar is half gone, there isn't pain anymore, and I can fuck. Yeah, I said it. Slutshame me all you want, but I've been waiting my whole life for this.

One morning last week, Devyn used their thigh to push fingers inside of me, and I was in ecstasy. The next day, Isaac came into town, and he was the first to go down on me. I convulsed so hard that I passed out twice. Aiden is more of a gentle lover, and has used a strap-on a couple times, but he's been on testosterone long enough that just rubbing himself against me gets him off. The getting is good.

I've still only experienced the one orgasm, but just the sensations I'm experiencing now are way better than any penile orgasm I ever had. Anti-trans activists love to quote statistics about how unhappy trans women supposedly are after getting their surgeries, but I don't know what the fuck they're talking about.

I refuse to feed into the cultural narrative of the sad gay or the sad trans. This is the trope that if we are represented at all, our entire existence is about being sad, oppressed, and facing violence. Y'all, every time I pee, I giggle to myself and say "teehee, I peed with my vagina!" I wear short skirts and skimpy dresses with no dysphoria about trying to hide the one part of me that doesn't match up with the rest. Despite Twitter comments when I appear on an atheist YouTube show, I am by far the happiest I've ever been. I'm in love with three amazing people, and I date even more than that.

Isaac, someone who has only been with women his entire life, said that my vagina has its own scent, taste, and is near indistinguishable from natal models. This is 12 weeks in. I still have scars. And he fucked me like there was no tomorrow. I don't care if that's TMI. I'm a trans woman with a vagina and I fuck. A lot. Men, women, and enbies like me for who I am, and enjoy my vagina as I enjoy whatever they have. I don't give a single shit if that makes you uncomfortable. I'm sick of holding back who I am so that others don't feel oppressed by my happiness with my own existence. It's 2018; if you still don't know anything about queer folx, at some point it's not our fucking problem.

The Trump Administration has since leaked a memo about trying to eliminate our identities from existence, and is still pushing for his ridiculous military ban now that he's stacked the Supreme Court in his favor. Yet, we're still here. We will fight anything he tries to pass to restrict us from being able to live fully as we are. I'm sure that it gives him a momentary distraction from all his cohorts getting arrested, but as long as he can jingle some keys about the queers, the YouTube comment section as a political base will happily do anything they can to make us miserable. I refuse to let them do so. We will not be erased.

My name is Marissa. I am a woman. You don't get to override that, nor are you entitled to your opinion. You do not know me better than I know myself. And even if it was a mental illness to be trans (it's not), do you really think a surgeon at the best hospital in the country would give me the surgery you're reading about right now based on a delusion? Go fuck yourself. Everyone is entitled to an opinion, but that doesn't mean yours deserves to be considered equally. You don't get to tell me I'm not a woman, because while you are perfectly entitled to be wrong, I don't have to give your dogshit opinions any weight, merit, or consideration. Go fuck yourself

This surgery is on a short list of the best decisions I've ever made. I am trans, and I am happy. Die mad about it.

Becoming My Own

By Hontas Farmer

Without going into my life story and state it plainly, for me sexual reassignment surgery was life affirming. My gender identity, that internal sense of how I fit into the human world is affirmed by how I live and interact with others. Surgery is just another way of doing that. It is not the ultimate way or the defining way that a subset of transgender people change our sexual anatomy. That said, while I could've lived without it, I would have regretted not doing it. Without telling my life story that is the sum and substance of what SRS was, and has been for me.

So, yeah you want to know more than that. WHAT WAS IT LIKE?

The actual surgery itself was not much of an experience. The medical team was introduced to me in the prep room. The surgical nurse, doctor, and his intern there to observe. Last but not least the anesthesiologist. Who came in and introduced himself. He said "Let me get this first cocktail into you". I'd swear to God he said it like Quagmire, a character from Family Guy. I was amused. I thought to myself of a panel from a very adult manga that summed up how I felt in that moment. "I can't turn back anymore. I don't want to turn back." Then nothing.....

.... Then I woke up in recovery not feeling much pain but my foot was asleep. That was the surgery.

Why did my thoughts turn to animated media? I don't know. Maybe because surgery is scary, and this was comforting to think about. Thinking over the details of the surgery are not something I want to concentrate on. If I could've been hit by a bolt of magic and turned completely and painlessness into a female version of myself without fundamentally changing who I am. I would've thanked almighty God.

I knew though that SRS was not magic. People will still be shitty. The world is the world. Most of my medical caregivers were professional if not friendly and called me by the right pronouns. Which if you have a job in a hospital that does SRS and work on the SRS ward caring for SRS patients should not be a big issue. Not all did they were reassigned. My family both lived up to what they promised and failed to. My jobs mostly did as one would expect of blue county purple state community colleges. Mostly, they accommodated my post surgical needs. The community college in deep blue Chicago gave me a problem while the one in purple redish DuPage county did not.

One thing straight people should realize is in practice when confronted with a living breathing transgender man or woman that is when you find out who's really liberal or conservative and what those labels mean to them. We can never assume and be 100% sure of how we will be treated anywhere...EVER.

Since then I have felt more than a foot that is asleep. Some pain in the incisions but otherwise not much. Surgery has quite simply made my body my own.

Beth's Journey

By Bethany Turner

I feel like such a fraud sometimes.

I wouldn't say I've had an easy life, but compared to some, I've coasted to where I am now. I've known people who've been conscious about their gender since they were teens or younger, but who are trapped in home environments where transitioning is simply untenable. I know people with health conditions that make transitioning medically difficult or even impossible. I've known people whose GIC has caused them years of delay, with all the torment of dysphoria that goes with it, because a cisgender doctor felt it was more important to deal with their numerous other, unrelated health issues before they'd give them the all clear them for surgery. I've known people who live with the fear that everything will be taken from them if they come out.

And look at me.

Six years ago, I wasn't even sure if I was trans yet. Now here I am, unemployed though I may be, nevertheless sat in a comfy chair, in a warm home, typing in front of a half decent computer, a little under fourteen months after having my own vagina installed. From initial diagnosis to the holy grail of gender confirmation surgery, my journey took only about four and a half years. Sure, my last employer gave me the sack because, much like Ris, I stood up for myself when I was misgendered; but flawed though it may be, the United Kingdom still has something resembling a decent welfare state. And even if I were to find myself evicted from my current home, my mother doesn't live far away and she would never see me homeless. All things considered, I've got it pretty good.

So I feel like a fraud.

I'm especially conscious of how difficult transitioning can be in the United States, if only through second hand accounts. The state-by-state regulations surrounding name changes, updating birth certificates, et cetera, the extreme expense of the process (even with

health insurance), and the constant growing shadow --
like a vast predatory bird, poised to strike -- of the current
regime's increasingly transphobic policies. At the time I
write this, it's about a week since the administration
announced its plans to essentially define transgender out
of existence via policy. Who the fuck knows what they'll
have done by the time this is published?

Conversely, when I was first coming to grips with
being a trans woman, over five years ago now, I learned
that hormones, surgery, even laser hair removal and voice
coaching would all be covered by the National Health
Service. And, since I live in Scotland, where prescription
drugs are free, I would essentially not have to pay a penny
towards my transition, except the occasional travel cost
for a consultation in Glasgow. Never much more than
£20.00 at a time for a train ticket from Edinburgh

Waverley. And what is our government doing about trans rights? Well, you'd think with the utter pig's ear Theresa May and her fractious Conservative minority government are making of Brexit right now, there'd be no time to think about expanding the rights of trans Britons or to even consider legal acknowledgement of non-binary people. But two public consultations have just recently been held on the matter; a highly successful one here in Scotland and one for England and Wales that TERFs evidently tried desperately to sabotage, but all signs indicate was also similarly successful.

I can almost the grinding teeth of American readers and you are right to grind your teeth. This is not fair. This is not right. If other countries can slowly, but steadily stumble their way into getting this right, why can't yours? Why can't that bastion of freedom -- the "greatest country in the world", the global hub of commerce and industry, the country that put human beings on the moon -- why can't America figure out how to treat transgender people as... well, people?

I'm holding on to a strand of optimism yet that says, America spent a long time taking one step forward and two steps back on marriage equality before finally doing the right thing only a little over three years ago now. So maybe it will be the same trans rights? But things are looking dark in America right now. I can understand a general lack of hope there and how to navigate out of the current darkness is beyond me. Let's just say, I can understand why Ris wanted to get her surgery when she did and why some of my other American trans siblings are starting to work on their exit strategies.

Three Years Ago

By Melina Rayna Barratt

Star-date: 2018.12.03 ER - Earth Reckoning

Transitional Recollections log:

Three years ago last night I realized I wanted to, needed to, and could transition. I placed my first order of some basics I would need late that night. My previous experience trying to be "just a cross dresser" as well as a failed attempt to transition ten years before made it really easy for me to know what I needed to get started. My second marriage was ending, I couldn't medically stay in the career tracks I had been working in. That age old question "where do you see yourself in ten years" had been heavy on my mind for several months. I had come to the conclusion that I had three possible answers: dead, dying, or doing well(medically). While generally that may be true for just about everyone, because of my cancer the dead or dying was waaaaay more likely than average but also far from certain. I choose to concentrate on the Doing Well possibility. I enrolled in college to start a new career track that would also be less impacted by my possible future health. After I gave one last effort at saving my marriage over thanksgiving/my-birthday I had to confront my image of the future without her. How did I want to see myself? I guess hearing my now friend Callie Wright on various podcasts I listened to had started to reawaken that which I had tried to bury. Three years ago today, I woke up to who I wanted to be.

Star-date: 2018.12.05 ER

Transitional Recollections log:

When first started thinking about transitioning, I thought about all the new medical advances, and the possibilities I couldn't find before. I thought about my health problems, my kids, my near future scholastic endeavors. I figured, with some dismay, that it would be best to wait until my kids were older, I finished school, and hopefully my cancer would be less of a problem. Three years down the road maybe I could start hormones. Hopefully I could at least be myself parts of some days each week, mainly safely at home. Once I got my breast forms I found it difficult, even traumatizing, to remove my bra for that would mean removing my breasts. I slept with them on, even showered a time or two bc of a special adhesive. I started finding ways to wear my preferred clothing, often hidden underneath. A number of times I changed in my car after an appointment before going home.

I found a trans Discord server and made many new friends, some I later met in person. One of whom was the very first person to say my new name out loud to me in real life, in a parking garage in downtown Orlando. A friend on Discord questioned my reasoned plan with a simple "Why? Why wait?" That got me thinking, I started researching my cancer with an eye to possible effects of HRT. I learned enough to believe my cancer treatment would not be negatively impacted by HRT. Around the same time I had listened to a podcast with a trans woman talking about the recently opened Gender Clinic at the Mayo Clinic, Rochester. I had been going to the Mayo Clinic, Jacksonville for my cancer treatment so I reached out to both the trans woman on the podcast and my

Endo-Oncologist at Jacksonville about trying to get a referral. The transwoman put me in touch with another trans woman who was the leader of the local support group and both became friends when I later traveled there. They gave me a script for blockers, and a few months later I returned to receive a script for Estrogen.

Around the time of the first trip North I came out to my teacher at school and started presenting part time when there. The second trip was between semesters, and when I came back I fully presented when at school and changed my "preferred name" in the school records. My college is advanced enough that was possible! My teacher commented that she had seen it; she was amazingly supportive, and one of if not the best teacher I have ever had.

Star-date 2015.12.06 ER

Transitional Recollections Log:

When I first started thinking about transition timeframes I figured 3-5 years before starting hormones, probably 2 years on HRT before going Full Time, and maybe eventually a few years after that I would be able to afford bottom surgery. I got on blockers at 4 months, hormones at around 6, and went Full Time at 8. That was July of 2016. The desire, the need to stop living a lie was like a wrecking ball to my initial ideas and plans. I once said "why would I want to go back to living that drab, monochrome life". There was so much to learn, to enjoy, and to try. I had to spend time figuring out who I really was, what did I really like, how do I really feel (about various different things, like men)?

I spent the remainder of 2016 working on school and politics, and myself. I met my best friend, finalized the divorce from my second wife, and at a party a friend hosted for the event I got to know the person who would later become my spouse and partner.

Star-date: 2018.12.14 ER

Transitional Recollections Log:

In 2016 I worked hard at politics, helped a few campaigns and managed one. I never believed Hillary would win, and I was terrified Trump would. When he did, I made the personal commitment to be even more involved in trying to make things better for transfolk in whatever capacity I could manage. So many of my friends found motivation to start, speed up, and/or finish their transitions. Most emphasized surgeries or legal documents. My insurance covered what I needed, but finding a surgeon that had the time to see me would have been difficult, and my cancer would likely complicate things enough I wasn't sure any surgeon would be agreeable. In March 2017 I spoke with a close friend in Rochester, MN and learned they had started doing bottom surgeries for Trans women at the Mayo Clinic up there. I knew that if anyone would operate on me, it would be them. I felt my long history with the Mayo Clinic might make the difference. I started calling, I already had appointments scheduled at the beginning of May, to get a consult added to the list. If I was going to have this done I really needed it to be in between Summer and Fall semesters so I could avoid missing a semester and losing financial aid for the time. For me, there was a six week window in which I could do this and it was quickly approaching.

The consult was straight and to the point, yes they could fit me in during that window. Letters were needed, they could provide the more in depth one, it was up to me to secure the second and they couldn't start the insurance pre-approval without it. The therapist I had been seeing, in part with this in mind, resisted, must to my alarm. Back and forth for a few weeks, she just didn't feel qualified! What was I to do?!? I reached out to a friend I had known for a while who was also a therapist and it turned out had written such letters before. "Let's get this done!" Was her response, much to my relief. The clock was ticking. If I couldn't get this approved on done within the next few weeks, my schedule would force it to wait at least a full year, and I had no way to know whether it would still be allowed at that point considering the people Trump was putting in charge of everything.

I got the letters in and Mayo submitted for pre-approval. They assured me it would get handled in time, but my surgery date was only a month out, and approvals could take as long as a month to get, if they even approved it! I've heard of some not getting approved bc of some minor problem. I had to buy plane tickets, and my budget was very limited. Friends had helped me financially in many way to make it possible to get all this done, what if I bought the tickets, flew up there, and then got denied for some minor thing and have everything pushed back a month or more? At one point Mayo had to resubmit with different coding, I was practically panicking. It was still possible, could still be done in time. I don't remember if the approval came right before or right after I had to commit to the plane tickets, but I got both.

Through all this much needed to be done, stuff needed to be bought, things needed to be handled and prepared. I was going to be gone for about 2 months. I had friends up there to stay with thankfully. Anticipating everything you will need for two months post-op is not simple. When the day came, ready or not I was going!

I prefer flights from Atlanta to Minneapolis. I have friends in Atlanta I like to see and stay with. Makes it easy to catch early morning flights. Whatever you do, avoid driving in Georgia at night in the rain. There are few if any reflectors to show you the lanes. Because I was going to be gone for so long I couldn't leave my car at my friends place and two months of parking fees wouldn't be cheap. A friend agreed to not only drive me up and to the airport, but pick me up again on my return. She is an amazing friend, one of many on this journey. A friend paid for my plane ticket, and I was out of money. I had just enough to get to where I was going. Returning home wouldn't be a problem because I'd have other money by then, but I was broke by the time I got to the airport.

When I went to check my suitcase, I found it had not been included in the ticket. If I remember right, they wouldn't take cash, which I had. Both my friend who paid for the ticket(I'm so grateful) and my spouse separately tried to wire/transfer money into one of my accounts so I could pay for the luggage, but that doesn't happen instantly. While waiting I also worked on getting the big suitcase to be under the weight limit, checking my bank account every couple minutes. I get to the point that it's too late to check, I call my friend to turn around to take it back, thinking about shipping it, while I rearrange what's in my carry-on to at least have the minimum to get me to the hospital. My friend shows up and takes the bag, and I got to the security line while watching the clock. I'm not sure I'm going to make it, start checking to make sure I have everything and…. my ID is missing! I had it when I was trying to check my bag! Now I'm starting to feel panic, I get out of line and try to retrace my steps; nothing. I start going through my bags in case I dropped it inside, bawling my eyes out because I know there is no way to make my flight, and without my ID I won't even be able to get another flight. I ask the attendants at luggage, they don't have it. Back to hunting around, an attendant finds me bc another had found it and went to the gate I was supposed to be at. Partially relieved, holding back my panic, I explain there is no way I can get on the flight in time and I had surgery in a few days. They told me not to worry, they would get me on another flight. I check my bank and the money was there! I called my friend to turn back around again while I went back to the ticket counter. They got me another flight a few hours later. Plenty of time to get my bag, check it, and get through security. Panic was replaced by nervousness, things seem to be solved but what else might happen?

Nothing, as it turned out. Everything else worked out, I landed, got my luggage and everything else went to plan. In March of 2017 I found a way I could have this surgery, and on July 31st it was done.

Star-date: 2018.12.04 ER

Personal log:

I took my spouse and step-kids to see Bohemian Rhapsody. For the past week I have been playing the album "Queen, Live at Wembley 86" to my stepson. I bought it when I was in high school. Two disc, two hours of non-stop performance of Queen, a year after the Live Aid Concert featured at the end of the movie, and, as I understand it, a year before Freddie Mercury was actually diagnosed with AIDS. In the movie Freddie says, as he is trying to make up with the rest of the band, "what if I don't have time?" implying a fatalistic sense he suspected his life was not going to be a long one. This really sticks with me, something I regularly feel. He lived for six more years after the end of the movie, five after my album was recorded, four after his diagnosis. I was about to turn 13 at the time he died; he was 35. I knew very little about him, or the band, before this year. As he was portrayed in the movie, there was so much I could relate too. For the second time, I cried for most of the entire second half of the movie.

45235220R00107

Made in the USA
Columbia, SC
23 December 2018